iPhone

Available
(directly from the A

- Contains all 1200 photos from th
- Search function to quickly find foods.
- Meal function with automatic calculator.
- Ability to add custom foods with values.
- Calendar to keep track of past meals.
- Always in your pocket.

Flashcards

- Set of 54 durable flashcards.
- Variety of common food & drinks.
- Picture & weight on front.
- Picture, weight, carbs & calories on reverse.
- One side blue, one side green for easy sorting.
- Complete with matching box.

Teaching Packs

Carbs & Cals Teaching Packs are available for hospitals and schools. They offer great value and contain:

- Copies of this book
- Set of 5 themed posters
- Powerpoint presentation
- Flashcards

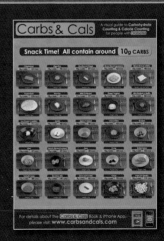

For more info please visit: **www.carbsandcals.com**

Contents

Introduction

Welcome to Carbs & Cals. This is a unique book, the likes of which has not been seen before. Unlike most books, there are lots of pictures and few words.

This book has been produced with two main purposes in mind; first and foremost it provides a fantastic resource for anyone with diabetes who is carbohydrate counting or thinking of learning to carb count. Secondly, for anyone who is trying to lose weight by counting calories or needs advice on portion control, it is a great visual reference to hundreds of different food items and drinks. For the first time, it gives you the ability to see photos of the portions you could choose, and how many calories you could save by making reductions in portion sizes or choosing lower calorie alternatives.

As this is primarily a carbohydrate counting book, foods with no or minimal carbohydrate content have not been included. These include meat, fish, eggs, cheese, oils & spreads, and some vegetables. We have included a large selection of popular food items, meals and drinks.

We hope you enjoy the book and that it makes the process of carbohydrate counting easier to understand.

What is carbohydrate?

Within our diets we have three main food groups. These are fat, protein and carbohydrate.

Carbohydrate foods provide the body with its main energy source, which is glucose. Carbohydrate is broken down by the body into glucose, which is then taken into our blood stream. The rate at which this happens depends on the type of carbohydrate eaten; this is known as the glycaemic index (GI). For example, white bread is readily broken down and causes a quick increase in blood glucose, whereas pasta is more slowly broken down, giving a more gradual increase.

For people contolling their diabetes with insulin, it is useful to have an understanding of the speed at which blood glucose may rise after certain meals or snacks. This can help you to predict your blood glucose level after eating or drinking. If you are adjusting insulin, speak to your diabetes team about this in more detail.

One of the main drawbacks of GI is that it does not take into account the other nutrients in the meal (e.g. protein and fat content), which can slow the absorption of glucose into the blood stream. It also fails to take into account the amount of carbohydrate in the meal, which is a much better predictor of blood glucose response. For people with diabetes, it is therefore important that they have an understanding of the total carbohydrate content of the food and drink they are consuming.

The table on the opposite page shows the main types of food that we eat that contain carbohydrate.

Food Group	Examples	Function
Starchy Foods	Bread, potato, rice, pasta, noodles, breakfast cereal, pastry, yam, cassava, pulses and grains e.g. cous cous	Provides fibre within the diet, especially wholegrain varieties. Also an important source of calcium, iron and B vitamins
Fruit & Vegetables	All types of fruit contain natural fruit sugar (fructose). Vegetables vary in the amount of carbohydrate they contain. Parsnips, butternut squash and other root vegetables generally contain higher amounts of carbs	A great source of vitamins, minerals and fibre within the diet
Dairy Foods	Milk, yoghurt, custard and ice cream all contain milk sugar (lactose)	Provides an important source of calcium, vitamins A and B12. Also contains a good source of protein
Sugary Foods	Sugar, jam, marmalade, honey, soft drinks, sweets, cakes, biscuits and chocolates	No nutritional benefits other than providing an energy source to the body

How much carbohydrate should I eat each day?

The amount of carbohydrate we should eat in a day varies from person to person depending on your activity levels, gender, age and weight. It is estimated that we should get around 50% of our energy from carbohydrate sources. No more than 35% should come from fat and around 10-20% should be from protein.

Within our diets, we have 5 main food groups. The Eatwell Plate shows how much of what you eat should come from each food group. This includes everything you eat during the day, including snacks. Try to eat plenty of fruit and vegetables, plenty of bread, rice, potatoes, pasta and other starchy foods (choose wholegrain varieties whenever you can), some milk and dairy foods, some meat, fish, eggs, beans and other non-dairy sources of protein, and just a small amount of food and drinks that are high in fat and/or sugar.

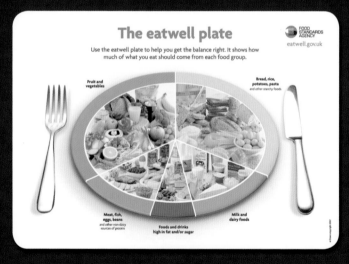

For people with diabetes, the current recommendation (from 2003), is that carbohydrate should make up 45-60% of energy intake. Diabetes UK is currently reviewing this recommendation and it is possible that scientific evidence may result in this value being amended in the future.

The table below shows the amount of carbohydrate per day for different calorie intakes based on 50% of energy:

Calories	Carbohydrate per day (based on 50% of calories)
1500 kcal	190g
2000 kcal	250g
2500 kcal	315g
3000 kcal	375g

Diabetes and Carbohydrate Counting

Carbohydrate counting for people with diabetes is not a new concept; it has been around for over 50 years. However, in recent years it has been incorporated more and more into the education and management of Type 1, Type 2 and diabetes in pregnancy.

Carbohydrate counting means being able to estimate the amount of carbohydrate in a meal, drink or snack by various means (e.g. estimating by sight, looking at food labels or weighing food items).

If you are starting out with carbohydrate counting, there are three main steps to consider:

1. Basic introduction to the concept of carbohydrate counting and understanding the amount of carbohydrate in the diet.

2. Understanding the relationships between food, diabetes medications, physical activity, and blood glucose level, and introducing the steps needed to manage these factors.

3. If you have Type 1 diabetes (and are using multiple daily injections or an insulin pump), learning how to match quick-acting insulin to carbohydrate, using carbohydrate-to-insulin ratios.

Learning to estimate the amount of carbohydrate can be hard work and very time-consuming; even experts in the field of diabetes can have difficulty in calculating carbohydrate. Eating out, take-away meals and dinner with friends can be especially challenging, as it is difficult to know what ingredients have been used and you may be eating foods you are not used to.

When we eat carbohydrate, whether it is pasta, bread, potato, fruit, milk or sugar, it is broken down in our stomachs into glucose. This glucose is then transferred into the blood stream and from there it is carried into cells of the body by the hormone insulin. The amount of insulin required is directly related to the total amount of carbohydrate in the meal or snack being eaten.

It is important to note that certain foods which are broken down into glucose very slowly may not require insulin or may require a reduced dose. This includes foods such as pearl barley, peas, beans and lentils, some vegetables including sweetcorn, squash/pumpkin and parsnips, and some fruit including cherries and grapefruit. It is important that you speak with your diabetes team about whether you may need to take insulin for these foods as it varies from person to person.

Due to the development of newer, quick-acting insulin such as Novorapid, Humalog and Apidra, adjusting the dose of insulin to the specific amount of carbohydrate in a meal has become possible. By adjusting insulin it is possible to have greater flexibility of food choice, reduced risk of hypoglycaemia and improved blood glucose control.

For people on multiple daily injections of insulin (basal bolus) or insulin pumps, knowing the amount of carbohydrate is important to make decisions about the amount of insulin to use. Many people on two injections a day find it useful to count carbohydrate in order to keep to similar amounts at each meal time.

In the UK, people with diabetes who are learning about carbohydrate counting are usually taught to take an amount of insulin based on each 10g of carbohydrate they eat. For example, many people are started on 1 unit of quick-acting insulin for every 10g of carbohydrate they consume. However, some people may need as much as 3 units or more per 10g of carbs. This rate will vary from person to person and can also vary at different times of the day. Your diabetes team can help to advise you on this. Please consult your diabetes centre if you require more information.

Learning how to adjust insulin and count carbohydrate can be complex. This book is not designed to teach you how to adjust your insulin regimen; it is important that you have the support of an appropriately trained health care professional such as a diabetes specialist nurse and dietitian.

Many areas of the UK now offer structured education courses such as BERTIE and DAFNE for Type 1 diabetes, and X-PERT and DESMOND for Type 2 diabetes. These courses can give a much greater insight into carbohydrate counting, as well as self-management of diabetes.

Diabetes and alcohol

Within this book, values have been included for alcoholic drinks that contain carbohydrate. These have been included as a reference only. Extreme caution should be taken when giving additional units of insulin with alcohol as you are more prone to hypoglycaemia (low blood glucose). Speak to your diabetes team about this in more detail.

What are calories?

Calories are units of energy. They are used to measure the amount of energy in the food and drink that we consume. This energy comes from the nutrients carbohydrate, fat, protein and alcohol.

Each of these nutrients contain a different number of calories per gram:

1g Carbohydrate	=	4 kcal
1g Fat	=	9 kcal
1g Protein	=	4 kcal
1g Alcohol	=	7 kcal

As seen above, fat has the most calories per gram. This is why if you eat a lot of foods that are high in fat, you will consume more calories and are likely to gain more weight.

People often associate carbohydrate with being 'fattening'. However as you can see above, carbohydrate contains the same calories per gram as protein. It is often the way people prepare the carbohydrate food (e.g. adding extra fat to a jacket potato, or frying) that increases the calorie content.

How many calories should I eat each day?

The amount of calories a person should eat or drink depends on a number of different factors. These include age, gender, physical activity levels and whether or not you are trying to lose, maintain or gain weight.

The guideline daily amount (GDA) of calories for a female is 2000, and 2500 for men. These figures are based on an average person. Sometimes GDAs are labelled 'for adults' - these figures are based on the GDA for women to encourage people who need less energy to consume fewer calories. People who are very active, overweight, or obese will have greater calorie requirements to maintain their current weight. It is possible to get a more accurate idea of your calorie needs per day by speaking to a registered dietitian.

Why count calories?

If you are trying to lose weight, it is useful to have an understanding of the calories contained in the food and drink you consume. It is also useful to have a realistic expectation of how many calories to cut down on and what weight loss you should expect.

Studies have shown that in order to lose 1lb of body weight over the course of a week, you need to reduce calories by around 500 per day (3500 per week). This reduction could be by diet alone, or by a combination of diet and increased physical activity. 500 calories is a large reduction, therefore it may be more beneficial to look at a 100-200 calorie reduction to start with.

By eating a slightly smaller portion, or going for a healthier snack, this should be more achievable. See below for an example of how you could save 336 calories by choosing a healthier snack option:

Chocolate Muffin		Strawberries	
55g CARBS	**404** CALS	**15**g CARBS	**68** CALS
Weight: 105g		Weight: 250g	

Advice on losing weight

Although the primary focus of this book is to look at carbohydrate counting, each picture also displays the calorie content. This provides a useful tool to track how many calories you are consuming in every meal or snack.

If you are trying to lose weight it is important to follow a balanced diet, including foods from all groups. You may wish to speak to a health care professional such as your GP, practice nurse or dietitian. If you have diabetes and take diabetes medication and/or insulin, weight loss may require a change in medication; it is best to seek medical advice first.

The British Dietetic Association (BDA) has developed a website (www.bdaweightwise.com) containing lots of useful hints and tips on losing weight. Diabetes UK (www.diabetes.org.uk) also has advice on weight loss, shopping tips and recipe ideas.

How to use this book

Carbs & Cals has been written with complete practicality in mind. The process of using the book is as follows:

1. Prepare your meal, drink or snack as normal.
2. Find the meal, drink or snack in the book.
3. Choose the portion photo that is closest to your own.
4. If you are carb counting, use the value in green above that photo, and if you are calorie counting, use the value in blue above that photo.
5. Add up the carb or calorie values for the different food components to give the totals for your meal.

All foods are displayed on one of the following dishes:

| 26cm Dinner Plate | 20cm Side Plate |
| 22cm Large Bowl | 14cm Cereal Bowl |

Each picture displays either a knife & fork, or a dessert spoon to help with scale. It may be a good idea to measure your own crockery to see how the size of your plates and bowls compares with the ones in the pictures, and possibly choose plates and bowls of a similar size to the ones shown to make it as easy as possible.

Foods are arranged in logical, alphabetical sections of Biscuits & Crackers, Bread, Breakfast, Cakes & Bakery Items, Desserts, Drinks, Fruit, Meals, Meal Accompaniments, Meat & Fish, Potatoes, Rice, Pasta & Grains, Snacks, Take-aways, and Vegetables & Pulses. The different sections are coloured so it's easy to find the food or drink you are looking for.

If you are eating a meal with multiple carbohydrate components (e.g. roast dinner, or cooked breakfast), you will need to find the various components in the book and add them up separately. For example, your roast dinner may comprise of Yorkshire puddings from page 152, stuffing from page 152, roast potatoes from page 171, parsnips from page 231, and cranberry sauce from page 153.

Each food has between 1 and 6 portion examples, so you can easily judge the carbs and cals in your particular portion just by looking at the different photos. For example, a digestive biscuit is always the same size, so only 1 photo has been included. However, there are 6 different portion pictures of lasagne included so that you can choose the portion that is closest to the portion on your plate.

The carb value is always in a large green tab, and the calorie value is in a large blue tab, so it's easy to see the values you are looking for.

50g CARBS   **326** CALS

The weight of each portion is stated underneath each photo, just in case you want to double-check the weight of your own portion. **This is always the cooked / prepared weight.**

Weight: 170g

For foods that you are likely to have several of, there is a table with the carbs and cals for 1, 2, 3 and 4 pieces, to make it even easier for you to add up.

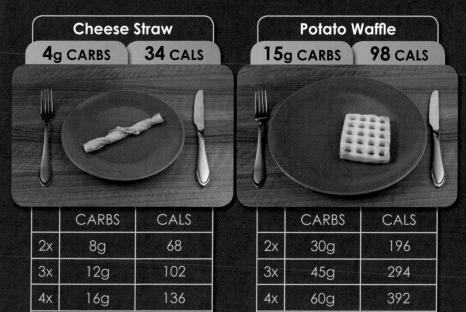

Cheese Straw

4g CARBS   **34** CALS

	CARBS	CALS
2x	8g	68
3x	12g	102
4x	16g	136
Weight: 7g		

Potato Waffle

15g CARBS   **98** CALS

	CARBS	CALS
2x	30g	196
3x	45g	294
4x	60g	392
Weight: 49g		

Bourbon Cream

8g CARBS | **59 CALS**

	CARBS	CALS
2x	16g	118
3x	24g	177
4x	32g	236
Weight: 12g		

Chocolate Digestive

10g CARBS | **74 CALS**

	CARBS	CALS
2x	20g	148
3x	30g	222
4x	40g	296
Weight: 15g		

Chocolate Chip Cookie

7g CARBS | **47 CALS**

	CARBS	CALS
2x	14g	94
3x	21g	141
4x	28g	188
Weight: 10g		

48g CARBS | **351 CALS**

	CARBS	CALS
2x	96g	702
3x	144g	1053
4x	192g	1404
Weight: 74g		

Chocolate Oat Biscuit

13g CARBS   **100 CALS**

	CARBS	CALS
2x	26g	200
3x	39g	300
4x	52g	400
Weight: 19g		

Custard Cream

8g CARBS   **58 CALS**

	CARBS	CALS
2x	16g	116
3x	24g	174
4x	32g	232
Weight: 12g		

Digestive

10g CARBS   **70 CALS**

	CARBS	CALS
2x	20g	140
3x	30g	210
4x	40g	280
Weight: 15g		

Fig Roll

15g CARBS   **80 CALS**

	CARBS	CALS
2x	30g	160
3x	45g	240
4x	60g	320
Weight: 21g		

Ginger Biscuit

8g CARBS   **44 CALS**

	CARBS	CALS
2x	16g	88
3x	24g	132
4x	32g	176
Weight: 10g		

Gingerbread Man

38g CARBS   **220 CALS**

	CARBS	CALS
2x	76g	440
3x	114g	660
4x	152g	880
Weight: 58g		

Iced Ring

5g CARBS   **27 CALS**

	CARBS	CALS
2x	10g	54
3x	15g	81
4x	20g	108
Weight: 6g		

Jaffa Cake

9g CARBS   **47 CALS**

	CARBS	CALS
2x	18g	94
3x	27g	141
4x	36g	188
Weight: 13g		

Jam Ring

13g CARBS　　**79** CALS

	CARBS	CALS
2x	26g	158
3x	39g	237
4x	52g	316
Weight: 18g		

Malted Milk

5g CARBS　　**39** CALS

	CARBS	CALS
2x	10g	78
3x	15g	117
4x	20g	156
Weight: 8g		

Nice

5g CARBS　　**39** CALS

	CARBS	CALS
2x	10g	78
3x	15g	117
4x	20g	156
Weight: 8g		

Oat Biscuit

10g CARBS　　**75** CALS

	CARBS	CALS
2x	20g	150
3x	30g	225
4x	40g	300
Weight: 16g		

Pink Wafer

6g CARBS	48 CALS

	CARBS	CALS
2x	12g	96
3x	18g	144
4x	24g	192
Weight: 9g		

Rich Tea

5g CARBS	33 CALS

	CARBS	CALS
2x	10g	66
3x	15g	99
4x	20g	132
Weight: 7g		

Shortbread Finger

10g CARBS	81 CALS

	CARBS	CALS
2x	20g	162
3x	30g	243
4x	40g	324
Weight: 16g		

Shortcake

7g CARBS	49 CALS

	CARBS	CALS
2x	14g	98
3x	21g	147
4x	28g	196
Weight: 10g		

Breadstick

4g CARBS | **21 CALS**

	CARBS	CALS
2x	8g	42
3x	12g	63
4x	16g	84

Weight: 5g

Cheddar

2g CARBS | **27 CALS**

	CARBS	CALS
2x	4g	54
3x	6g	81
4x	8g	108

Weight: 5g

Cheese Straw

4g CARBS | **34 CALS**

	CARBS	CALS
2x	8g	68
3x	12g	102
4x	16g	136

Weight: 7g

Cream Cracker

5g CARBS | **35 CALS**

	CARBS	CALS
2x	10g	70
3x	15g	105
4x	20g	140

Weight: 8g

Crispbread (thin)

4g CARBS   **19** CALS

	CARBS	CALS
2x	8g	38
3x	12g	57
4x	16g	76
Weight: 6g		

Crispbread

8g CARBS   **35** CALS

	CARBS	CALS
2x	16g	70
3x	24g	105
4x	32g	140
Weight: 11g		

Digestive (savoury)

9g CARBS   **85** CALS

	CARBS	CALS
2x	18g	170
3x	27g	255
4x	36g	340
Weight: 13g		

Oatcake

6g CARBS   **44** CALS

	CARBS	CALS
2x	12g	88
3x	18g	132
4x	24g	176
Weight: 10g		

Puffed Cracker

5g CARBS   **48 CALS**

	CARBS	CALS
2x	10g	96
3x	15g	144
4x	20g	192
Weight: 9g		

Rice Cake

6g CARBS   **30 CALS**

	CARBS	CALS
2x	12g	60
3x	18g	90
4x	24g	120
Weight: 8g		

Water Biscuit

4g CARBS   **24 CALS**

	CARBS	CALS
2x	8g	48
3x	12g	72
4x	16g	96
Weight: 6g		

Wholegrain Cracker

5g CARBS   **34 CALS**

	CARBS	CALS
2x	10g	68
3x	15g	102
4x	20g	136
Weight: 8g		

Sliced Bread (granary)

| 5g CARBS | 26 CALS |

Weight: 11g (thin slice)

| 10g CARBS | 52 CALS |

Weight: 22g (thin slice)

| 16g CARBS | 78 CALS |

Weight: 33g (medium slice)

| 21g CARBS | 104 CALS |

Weight: 44g (thick slice)

| 30g CARBS | 152 CALS |

Weight: 64g (extra thick slice)

| 41g CARBS | 204 CALS |

Weight: 86g

Sliced Bread (white)

5g CARBS	24 CALS

Weight: 11g (thin slice)

10g CARBS	48 CALS

Weight: 22g (thin slice)

15g CARBS	72 CALS

Weight: 33g (medium slice)

20g CARBS	94 CALS

Weight: 43g (thick slice)

30g CARBS	140 CALS

Weight: 64g (extra thick slice)

39g CARBS	186 CALS

Weight: 85g

Sliced Bread (wholemeal)

5g CARBS   24 CALS

Weight: 11g (thin slice)

10g CARBS   50 CALS

Weight: 23g (thin slice)

15g CARBS   78 CALS

Weight: 36g (medium slice)

21g CARBS   106 CALS

Weight: 49g (thick slice)

30g CARBS   154 CALS

Weight: 71g (extra thick slice)

40g CARBS   206 CALS

Weight: 95g

Bap (white)

25g CARBS	122 CALS	60g CARBS	295 CALS

Weight: 48g · Weight: 116g

Bap (wholemeal)

24g CARBS	124 CALS	53g CARBS	278 CALS

Weight: 51g · Weight: 114g

Crusty Roll (white)

25g CARBS	120 CALS	50g CARBS	241 CALS

Weight: 43g · Weight: 86g

Bagel

50g CARBS   **235** CALS

Weight: 86g

Burger Bun

40g CARBS   **216** CALS

Weight: 82g

Finger Roll

20g CARBS   **105** CALS

Weight: 41g

Poppy Seeded Roll

30g CARBS   **149** CALS

Weight: 54g

Pitta Bread

40g CARBS   **183** CALS

Weight: 69g

Pitta Bread (mini)

20g CARBS   **93** CALS

Weight: 35g

Ciabatta

50g CARBS | **263** CALS

Weight: 97g

Panini

45g CARBS | **272** CALS

Weight: 100g

French Stick (slice)

20g CARBS | **100** CALS

Weight: 37g

French Stick (small)

65g CARBS | **319** CALS

Weight: 118g

Garlic Bread

10g CARBS | **80** CALS

Weight: 22g

30g CARBS | **241** CALS

Weight: 66g

Crumpet

20g CARBS **90 CALS**

Weight: 45g

Crumpet (square)

25g CARBS **113 CALS**

Weight: 57g

English Muffin

30g CARBS **152 CALS**

Weight: 68g

Tea Cake

50g CARBS **280 CALS**

Weight: 85g

Tortilla

35g CARBS **152 CALS**

Weight: 58g

Turkish Flatbread

30g CARBS **157 CALS**

Weight: 60g

Naan Bread

70g CARBS | **399** CALS

Weight: 140g

Naan Bread (mini)

30g CARBS | **171** CALS

Weight: 60g

Chapati

20g CARBS | **91** CALS

Weight: 45g

Paratha

40g CARBS | **297** CALS

Weight: 92g

Poppadom (small)

4g CARBS | **65** CALS

Weight: 13g

Poppadom (large)

7g CARBS | **125** CALS

Weight: 25g

Brioche

| 10g CARBS | 64 CALS | 25g CARBS | 159 CALS |

Weight: 18g   Weight: 45g

Croissant

| 11g CARBS | 97 CALS | 22g CARBS | 190 CALS |

Weight: 26g   Weight: 51g

Pain au Chocolat

| 14g CARBS | 142 CALS | 27g CARBS | 267 CALS |

Weight: 32g   Weight: 64g

Toast with Chocolate Spread & Margarine

7g CARBS   57 CALS

	CARBS	CALS
2x	14g	114
3x	21g	171
4x	28g	228

Weight: 13g (thin slice)

13g CARBS   112 CALS

	CARBS	CALS
2x	26g	224
3x	39g	336
4x	52g	448

Weight: 26g (thin slice)

18g CARBS   136 CALS

	CARBS	CALS
2x	36g	272
3x	54g	408
4x	72g	544

Weight: 36g (medium slice)

23g CARBS   158 CALS

	CARBS	CALS
2x	46g	316
3x	69g	474
4x	92g	632

Weight: 46g (thick slice)

Toast with Honey & Margarine

7g CARBS   50 CALS

	CARBS	CALS
2x	14g	100
3x	21g	150
4x	28g	200
Weight: 13g (thin slice)		

14g CARBS   99 CALS

	CARBS	CALS
2x	28g	198
3x	42g	297
4x	56g	396
Weight: 26g (thin slice)		

19g CARBS   123 CALS

	CARBS	CALS
2x	38g	246
3x	57g	369
4x	76g	492
Weight: 36g (medium slice)		

24g CARBS   145 CALS

	CARBS	CALS
2x	48g	290
3x	72g	435
4x	96g	580
Weight: 46g (thick slice)		

Toast with Jam & Margarine

7g CARBS   50 CALS

	CARBS	CALS
2x	14g	100
3x	21g	150
4x	28g	200
Weight: 13g (thin slice)		

13g CARBS   98 CALS

	CARBS	CALS
2x	26g	196
3x	39g	294
4x	52g	392
Weight: 26g (thin slice)		

18g CARBS   122 CALS

	CARBS	CALS
2x	36g	244
3x	54g	366
4x	72g	488
Weight: 36g (medium slice)		

23g CARBS   144 CALS

	CARBS	CALS
2x	46g	288
3x	69g	432
4x	92g	576
Weight: 46g (thick slice)		

Toast with Lemon Curd & Margarine

7g CARBS   50 CALS

	CARBS	CALS
2x	14g	100
3x	21g	150
4x	28g	200
Weight: 13g (thin slice)		

13g CARBS   99 CALS

	CARBS	CALS
2x	26g	198
3x	39g	297
4x	52g	396
Weight: 26g (thin slice)		

18g CARBS   123 CALS

	CARBS	CALS
2x	36g	246
3x	54g	369
4x	72g	492
Weight: 36g (medium slice)		

23g CARBS   145 CALS

	CARBS	CALS
2x	46g	290
3x	69g	435
4x	92g	580
Weight: 46g (thick slice)		

Toast with Marmalade & Margarine

7g CARBS   **50 CALS**

	CARBS	CALS
2x	14g	100
3x	21g	150
4x	28g	200
Weight: 13g (thin slice)		

13g CARBS   **98 CALS**

	CARBS	CALS
2x	26g	196
3x	39g	294
4x	52g	392
Weight: 26g (thin slice)		

18g CARBS   **122 CALS**

	CARBS	CALS
2x	36g	244
3x	54g	366
4x	72g	488
Weight: 36g (medium slice)		

23g CARBS   **144 CALS**

	CARBS	CALS
2x	46g	288
3x	69g	432
4x	92g	576
Weight: 46g (thick slice)		

Toast with Peanut Butter & Margarine

5g CARBS   58 CALS

	CARBS	CALS
2x	10g	116
3x	15g	174
4x	20g	232
Weight: 13g (thin slice)		

11g CARBS   115 CALS

	CARBS	CALS
2x	22g	230
3x	33g	345
4x	44g	460
Weight: 26g (thin slice)		

16g CARBS   139 CALS

	CARBS	CALS
2x	32g	278
3x	48g	417
4x	64g	556
Weight: 36g (medium slice)		

21g CARBS   161 CALS

	CARBS	CALS
2x	42g	322
3x	63g	483
4x	84g	644
Weight: 46g (thick slice)		

Bran Flakes

10g CARBS   **50 CALS**

Weight: 15g

20g CARBS   **99 CALS**

Weight: 30g

30g CARBS   **149 CALS**

Weight: 45g

40g CARBS   **198 CALS**

Weight: 60g

50g CARBS   **248 CALS**

Weight: 75g

60g CARBS   **300 CALS**

Weight: 91g

Chocolate Snaps

10g CARBS	42 CALS

Weight: 11g

19g CARBS	80 CALS

Weight: 21g

29g CARBS	123 CALS

Weight: 32g

38g CARBS	161 CALS

Weight: 42g

48g CARBS	203 CALS

Weight: 53g

59g CARBS	245 CALS

Weight: 64g

Corn Flakes

11g CARBS   **45** CALS

Weight: 12g

21g CARBS   **86** CALS

Weight: 23g

31g CARBS   **132** CALS

Weight: 35g

42g CARBS   **177** CALS

Weight: 47g

52g CARBS   **218** CALS

Weight: 58g

63g CARBS   **263** CALS

Weight: 70g

Fruit & Fibre

10g CARBS   56 CALS

Weight: 15g

20g CARBS   107 CALS

Weight: 29g

30g CARBS   163 CALS

Weight: 44g

40g CARBS   218 CALS

Weight: 59g

50g CARBS   270 CALS

Weight: 73g

60g CARBS   326 CALS

Weight: 88g

Honey Puffed Wheat

10g CARBS   **45 CALS**

Weight: 12g

20g CARBS   **87 CALS**

Weight: 23g

30g CARBS   **133 CALS**

Weight: 35g

40g CARBS   **178 CALS**

Weight: 47g

50g CARBS   **220 CALS**

Weight: 58g

60g CARBS   **265 CALS**

Weight: 70g

Malted Wheats

10g CARBS	48 CALS

Weight: 14g

20g CARBS	95 CALS

Weight: 28g

30g CARBS	143 CALS

Weight: 42g

40g CARBS	190 CALS

Weight: 56g

50g CARBS	238 CALS

Weight: 70g

60g CARBS	286 CALS

Weight: 84g

Muesli

20g CARBS **110** CALS

Weight: 30g

40g CARBS **220** CALS

Weight: 60g

60g CARBS **329** CALS

Weight: 90g

80g CARBS **436** CALS

Weight: 119g

100g CARBS **545** CALS

Weight: 149g

120g CARBS **655** CALS

Weight: 179g

Multigrain Hoops

10g CARBS   **48** CALS

Weight: 13g

15g CARBS   **73** CALS

Weight: 20g

20g CARBS   **99** CALS

Weight: 27g

25g CARBS   **121** CALS

Weight: 33g

30g CARBS   **147** CALS

Weight: 40g

35g CARBS   **172** CALS

Weight: 47g

Porridge (made with whole milk)

9g CARBS	85 CALS

Weight: 75g

18g CARBS	164 CALS

Weight: 145g

28g CARBS	249 CALS

Weight: 220g

37g CARBS	328 CALS

Weight: 290g

46g CARBS	412 CALS

Weight: 365g

55g CARBS	492 CALS

Weight: 435g

Raisin Bites

15g CARBS   **72 CALS**

Weight: 22g

30g CARBS   **144 CALS**

Weight: 44g

45g CARBS   **213 CALS**

Weight: 65g

60g CARBS   **284 CALS**

Weight: 87g

75g CARBS   **353 CALS**

Weight: 108g

90g CARBS   **425 CALS**

Weight: 130g

Rice Snaps

10g CARBS   42 CALS

Weight: 11g

20g CARBS   88 CALS

Weight: 23g

30g CARBS   130 CALS

Weight: 34g

40g CARBS   176 CALS

Weight: 46g

50g CARBS   218 CALS

Weight: 57g

60g CARBS   264 CALS

Weight: 69g

Special Flakes with Berries

10g CARBS **47 CALS**

Weight: 13g

20g CARBS **95 CALS**

Weight: 26g

30g CARBS **146 CALS**

Weight: 40g

40g CARBS **193 CALS**

Weight: 53g

50g CARBS **241 CALS**

Weight: 66g

60g CARBS **292 CALS**

Weight: 80g

Wheat Biscuit

13g CARBS	64 CALS

	CARBS	CALS
2x	26g	128
3x	39g	192
4x	52g	256
Weight: 19g		

Wheat Pillow

15g CARBS	75 CALS

	CARBS	CALS
2x	30g	150
3x	45g	225
4x	60g	300
Weight: 22g		

Oat Biscuit

13g CARBS	75 CALS

	CARBS	CALS
2x	26g	150
3x	39g	225
4x	52g	300
Weight: 20g		

Milk (semi-skimmed)

5g CARBS	46 CALS

	CARBS	CALS
2x	10g	92
3x	15g	138
4x	20g	184
Weight: 100g		

Eggy Bread

| 5g CARBS | 97 CALS | | 10g CARBS | 193 CALS |

	CARBS	CALS
2x	10g	194
3x	15g	291
4x	20g	388
Weight: 25g (thin slice)		

	CARBS	CALS
2x	20g	386
3x	30g	579
4x	40g	772
Weight: 50g (thin slice)		

Fried Bread

| 5g CARBS | 80 CALS | | 10g CARBS | 160 CALS |

	CARBS	CALS
2x	10g	160
3x	15g	240
4x	20g	320
Weight: 15g (thin slice)		

	CARBS	CALS
2x	20g	320
3x	30g	480
4x	40g	640
Weight: 30g (thin slice)		

Breakfast Tart

35g CARBS   **205 CALS**

	CARBS	CALS
2x	70g	410
3x	105g	615
4x	140g	820
Weight: 52g		

Scotch Pancake

15g CARBS   **87 CALS**

	CARBS	CALS
2x	- 30g	174
3x	45g	261
4x	60g	348
Weight: 31g		

Waffle (sweet)

20g CARBS   **166 CALS**

	CARBS	CALS
2x	40g	332
3x	60g	498
4x	80g	664
Weight: 38g		

30g CARBS   **258 CALS**

	CARBS	CALS
2x	60g	516
3x	90g	774
4x	120g	1032
Weight: 59g		

Pancake (plain)

5g CARBS   60 CALS

	CARBS	CALS
2x	10g	120
3x	15g	180
4x	20g	240
Weight: 22g		

10g CARBS   117 CALS

	CARBS	CALS
2x	20g	234
3x	30g	351
4x	40g	468
Weight: 43g		

15g CARBS   169 CALS

	CARBS	CALS
2x	30g	338
3x	45g	507
4x	60g	676
Weight: 62g		

20g CARBS   232 CALS

	CARBS	CALS
2x	40g	464
3x	60g	696
4x	80g	928
Weight: 85g		

Pancake with Chocolate Spread

10g CARBS | 104 CALS

	CARBS	CALS
2x	20g	208
3x	30g	312
4x	40g	416
Weight: 30g		

15g CARBS | 161 CALS

	CARBS	CALS
2x	30g	322
3x	45g	483
4x	60g	644
Weight: 51g		

25g CARBS | 257 CALS

	CARBS	CALS
2x	50g	514
3x	75g	771
4x	100g	1028
Weight: 78g		

30g CARBS | 320 CALS

	CARBS	CALS
2x	60g	640
3x	90g	960
4x	120g	1280
Weight: 101g		

Pancake with Maple Syrup

10g CARBS | **81 CALS**

	CARBS	CALS
2x	20g	162
3x	30g	243
4x	40g	324
Weight: 30g		

15g CARBS | **138 CALS**

	CARBS	CALS
2x	30g	276
3x	45g	414
4x	60g	552
Weight: 51g		

25g CARBS | **211 CALS**

	CARBS	CALS
2x	50g	422
3x	75g	633
4x	100g	844
Weight: 78g		

30g CARBS | **274 CALS**

	CARBS	CALS
2x	60g	548
3x	90g	822
4x	120g	1096
Weight: 101g		

Pancake with Sugar & Lemon

10g CARBS   80 CALS

	CARBS	CALS
2x	20g	160
3x	30g	240
4x	40g	320
Weight: 22g		

15g CARBS   137 CALS

	CARBS	CALS
2x	30g	274
3x	45g	411
4x	60g	548
Weight: 43g		

25g CARBS   209 CALS

	CARBS	CALS
2x	50g	418
3x	75g	627
4x	100g	836
Weight: 62g		

30g CARBS   272 CALS

	CARBS	CALS
2x	60g	544
3x	90g	816
4x	120g	1088
Weight: 85g		

Greek Yoghurt

4g CARBS | **113** CALS

Weight: 85g

Natural Yoghurt

5g CARBS | **55** CALS

Weight: 70g

8g CARBS | **226** CALS

Weight: 170g

15g CARBS | **150** CALS

Weight: 190g

12g CARBS | **346** CALS

Weight: 260g

25g CARBS | **253** CALS

Weight: 320g

Baklava

8g CARBS   **64 CALS**

	CARBS	CALS
2x	16g	128
3x	24g	192
4x	32g	256
Weight: 20g		

11g CARBS   **90 CALS**

	CARBS	CALS
2x	22g	180
3x	33g	270
4x	44g	360
Weight: 28g		

6g CARBS   **45 CALS**

	CARBS	CALS
2x	12g	90
3x	18g	135
4x	24g	180
Weight: 14g		

10g CARBS   **84 CALS**

	CARBS	CALS
2x	20g	168
3x	30g	252
4x	40g	336
Weight: 26g		

Bakewell Tart

15g CARBS	155 CALS

Weight: 34g

20g CARBS	205 CALS

Weight: 45g

40g CARBS	424 CALS

Weight: 93g

Carrot Cake

20g CARBS	190 CALS

Weight: 53g

40g CARBS	384 CALS

Weight: 107g

60g CARBS	578 CALS

Weight: 161g

Chocolate Cake

20g CARBS   **186** CALS

Weight: 40g

35g CARBS   **325** CALS

Weight: 70g

70g CARBS   **640** CALS

Weight: 138g

Fruit Cake

15g CARBS   **92** CALS

Weight: 26g

35g CARBS   **212** CALS

Weight: 60g

70g CARBS   **428** CALS

Weight: 121g

Ginger Cake

15g CARBS   **91 CALS**

Weight: 24g

25g CARBS   **152 CALS**

Weight: 40g

35g CARBS   **213 CALS**

Weight: 56g

Malt Loaf

20g CARBS   **93 CALS**

Weight: 30g

40g CARBS   **189 CALS**

Weight: 61g

60g CARBS   **282 CALS**

Weight: 91g

Swiss Roll

20g CARBS	118 CALS

Weight: 35g

40g CARBS	233 CALS

Weight: 69g

60g CARBS	347 CALS

Weight: 103g

Victoria Sponge

20g CARBS	158 CALS

Weight: 44g

35g CARBS	277 CALS

Weight: 77g

70g CARBS	558 CALS

Weight: 155g

Apple Danish

45g CARBS   **298** CALS

Weight: 87g

Choc Chip Twist

40g CARBS   **357** CALS

Weight: 85g

Cinnamon Swirl

40g CARBS   **285** CALS

Weight: 79g

Fruit Trellis

20g CARBS   **152** CALS

Weight: 58g

Pain au Raisin

35g CARBS   **273** CALS

Weight: 95g

Pecan Plait

35g CARBS   **365** CALS

Weight: 81g

Chocolate Éclair

15g CARBS   **222** CALS

Weight: 56g

Corn Flake Cake

10g CARBS   **251** CALS

Weight: 54g

Cup Cake

40g CARBS   **199** CALS

Weight: 56g

Custard Slice

40g CARBS   **314** CALS

Weight: 106g

Custard Tart

30g CARBS   **255** CALS

Weight: 92g

Mini Battenburg

15g CARBS   **111** CALS

Weight: 30g

Choc Ring Doughnut

25g CARBS | **201** CALS

Weight: 49g

Glazed Ring Doughnut

25g CARBS | **176** CALS

Weight: 46g

Jam Doughnut

35g CARBS | **239** CALS

Weight: 71g

Mini Doughnut

5g CARBS | **44** CALS

Weight: 11g

Sprinkle Ring Doughnut

25g CARBS | **212** CALS

Weight: 58g

Sugar Ring Doughnut

30g CARBS | **263** CALS

Weight: 66g

Fresh Cream Doughnut

25g CARBS   **228** CALS

Weight: 69g

Yum Yum

35g CARBS   **293** CALS

Weight: 70g

Blueberry Muffin

12g CARBS   **86** CALS

Weight: 25g

48g CARBS   **353** CALS

Weight: 102g

Chocolate Muffin

15g CARBS   **108** CALS

Weight: 28g

55g CARBS   **404** CALS

Weight: 105g

Flapjack

30g CARBS	242 CALS

Weight: 50g

50g CARBS	397 CALS

Weight: 82g

Meringue Nest

5g CARBS	19 CALS

Weight: 5g

15g CARBS	61 CALS

Weight: 16g

Mince Pie

25g CARBS	178 CALS

Weight: 42g

35g CARBS	254 CALS

Weight: 60g

Belgian Bun

65g CARBS   **419** CALS

Weight: 116g

Cheese Scone

25g CARBS   **238** CALS

Weight: 68g

Fruit Scone

20g CARBS   **120** CALS

Weight: 38g

35g CARBS   **209** CALS

Weight: 66g

Hot Cross Bun

30g CARBS   **158** CALS

Weight: 51g

Iced Bun

20g CARBS   **124** CALS

Weight: 37g

Apple Pie

20g CARBS   **141 CALS**

Weight: 50g

40g CARBS   **282 CALS**

Weight: 100g

60g CARBS   **426 CALS**

Weight: 151g

80g CARBS   **567 CALS**

Weight: 201g

100g CARBS   **711 CALS**

Weight: 252g

120g CARBS   **852 CALS**

Weight: 302g

Apple & Rhubarb Crumble

22g CARBS   **131 CALS**

Weight: 60g

42g CARBS   **256 CALS**

Weight: 117g

63g CARBS   **383 CALS**

Weight: 175g

85g CARBS   **515 CALS**

Weight: 235g

106g CARBS   **646 CALS**

Weight: 295g

127g CARBS   **771 CALS**

Weight: 352g

Apple Strudel

15g CARBS   **126 CALS**

Weight: 45g

30g CARBS   **252 CALS**

Weight: 90g

45g CARBS   **378 CALS**

Weight: 135g

60g CARBS   **510 CALS**

Weight: 182g

75g CARBS   **638 CALS**

Weight: 228g

90g CARBS   **762 CALS**

Weight: 272g

Banoffee Pie

20g CARBS **146 CALS**

Weight: 43g

40g CARBS **303 CALS**

Weight: 89g

60g CARBS **452 CALS**

Weight: 133g

80g CARBS **598 CALS**

Weight: 176g

100g CARBS **748 CALS**

Weight: 220g

120g CARBS **901 CALS**

Weight: 265g

Black Forest Gateau

10g CARBS   **90 CALS**

Weight: 35g

20g CARBS   **175 CALS**

Weight: 68g

30g CARBS   **257 CALS**

Weight: 100g

40g CARBS   **347 CALS**

Weight: 135g

50g CARBS   **432 CALS**

Weight: 168g

60g CARBS   **514 CALS**

Weight: 200g

Bread & Butter Pudding

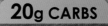

| 10g CARBS | 98 CALS | 20g CARBS | 199 CALS |

Weight: 40g   Weight: 81g

| 30g CARBS | 300 CALS | 40g CARBS | 403 CALS |

Weight: 122g   Weight: 164g

| 50g CARBS | 504 CALS | 60g CARBS | 605 CALS |

Weight: 205g   Weight: 246g

Brownie

25g CARBS   **200 CALS**

Weight: 45g

45g CARBS   **364 CALS**

Weight: 82g

70g CARBS   **564 CALS**

Weight: 127g

90g CARBS   **728 CALS**

Weight: 164g

115g CARBS   **928 CALS**

Weight: 209g

135g CARBS   **1092 CALS**

Weight: 246g

Cheesecake

18g CARBS | **147 CALS**

Weight: 50g

35g CARBS | **294 CALS**

Weight: 100g

53g CARBS | **441 CALS**

Weight: 150g

70g CARBS | **588 CALS**

Weight: 200g

88g CARBS | **735 CALS**

Weight: 250g

106g CARBS | **882 CALS**

Weight: 300g

Chocolate Torte

10g CARBS   **107 CALS**

Weight: 33g

20g CARBS   **215 CALS**

Weight: 66g

30g CARBS   **325 CALS**

Weight: 100g

40g CARBS   **432 CALS**

Weight: 133g

50g CARBS   **540 CALS**

Weight: 166g

60g CARBS   **650 CALS**

Weight: 200g

Christmas Pudding

20g CARBS **115 CALS**

Weight: 35g

40g CARBS **234 CALS**

Weight: 71g

60g CARBS **349 CALS**

Weight: 106g (individual)

80g CARBS **467 CALS**

Weight: 142g

100g CARBS **582 CALS**

Weight: 177g

120g CARBS **704 CALS**

Weight: 214g

Custard (made with whole milk)

10g CARBS   70 CALS

Weight: 60g

20g CARBS   140 CALS

Weight: 120g

30g CARBS   211 CALS

Weight: 180g

40g CARBS   281 CALS

Weight: 240g

50g CARBS   351 CALS

Weight: 300g

60g CARBS   421 CALS

Weight: 360g

Ice Cream (vanilla)

8g CARBS   **71 CALS**

Weight: 40g

Lemon Sorbet

15g CARBS   **59 CALS**

Weight: 45g

16g CARBS   **142 CALS**

Weight: 80g

30g CARBS   **115 CALS**

Weight: 88g

24g CARBS   **214 CALS**

Weight: 121g

45g CARBS   **173 CALS**

Weight: 132g

Choc Ice

15g CARBS | **144 CALS**

Weight: 52g

Crème Brûlée

15g CARBS | **343 CALS**

Weight: 104g

Chocolate & Nut Cone

25g CARBS | **190 CALS**

Weight: 73g

Panna Cotta

25g CARBS | **413 CALS**

Weight: 145g

Ice Cream Lolly

25g CARBS | **308 CALS**

Weight: 89g

Strawberry Tartlet

35g CARBS | **330 CALS**

Weight: 132g

Jelly

10g CARBS   **40 CALS**

Weight: 65g

20g CARBS   **79 CALS**

Weight: 130g

30g CARBS   **122 CALS**

Weight: 200g

40g CARBS   **162 CALS**

Weight: 265g

50g CARBS   **201 CALS**

Weight: 330g

60g CARBS   **244 CALS**

Weight: 400g

Lemon Meringue Pie

20g CARBS | **140 CALS**

Weight: 44g

40g CARBS | **281 CALS**

Weight: 88g

60g CARBS | **415 CALS**

Weight: 130g

80g CARBS | **558 CALS**

Weight: 175g

100g CARBS | **695 CALS**

Weight: 218g

120g CARBS | **836 CALS**

Weight: 262g

Mousse (chocolate)

10g CARBS   **70** CALS

Weight: 50g

20g CARBS   **139** CALS

Weight: 100g

30g CARBS   **209** CALS

Weight: 150g

40g CARBS   **278** CALS

Weight: 200g

50g CARBS   **348** CALS

Weight: 250g

60g CARBS   **417** CALS

Weight: 300g

Profiteroles

10g CARBS   **138** CALS

Weight: 40g

20g CARBS   **277** CALS

Weight: 80g

30g CARBS   **415** CALS

Weight: 120g

40g CARBS   **557** CALS

Weight: 161g

50g CARBS   **709** CALS

Weight: 205g

60g CARBS   **848** CALS

Weight: 245g

Rice Pudding

10g CARBS   **62 CALS**

Weight: 70g

20g CARBS   **125 CALS**

Weight: 140g

30g CARBS   **191 CALS**

Weight: 215g

40g CARBS   **254 CALS**

Weight: 285g

50g CARBS   **316 CALS**

Weight: 355g

60g CARBS   **378 CALS**

Weight: 425g

Roulade

20g CARBS   **133 CALS**

Weight: 38g

40g CARBS   **266 CALS**

Weight: 76g

60g CARBS   **399 CALS**

Weight: 114g

80g CARBS   **539 CALS**

Weight: 154g

100g CARBS   **672 CALS**

Weight: 192g

120g CARBS   **805 CALS**

Weight: 230g

Spotted Dick

25g CARBS   **180 CALS**

Weight: 52g

50g CARBS   **363 CALS**

Weight: 105g (individual)

75g CARBS   **547 CALS**

Weight: 158g

100g CARBS   **730 CALS**

Weight: 211g

125g CARBS   **913 CALS**

Weight: 264g

150g CARBS   **1097 CALS**

Weight: 317g

Sticky Toffee Pudding

15g CARBS   112 CALS

Weight: 31g

30g CARBS   223 CALS

Weight: 62g

45g CARBS   338 CALS

Weight: 94g

60g CARBS   450 CALS

Weight: 125g

75g CARBS   569 CALS

Weight: 158g

90g CARBS   680 CALS

Weight: 189g

Strawberry Delight

5g CARBS	38 CALS

Weight: 33g

15g CARBS	116 CALS

Weight: 100g

25g CARBS	193 CALS

Weight: 166g

35g CARBS	270 CALS

Weight: 233g

45g CARBS	348 CALS

Weight: 300g

55g CARBS	427 CALS

Weight: 368g

Summer Pudding

10g CARBS   **43 CALS**

Weight: 45g

20g CARBS   **89 CALS**

Weight: 94g

30g CARBS   **133 CALS**

Weight: 140g (individual)

40g CARBS   **176 CALS**

Weight: 185g

50g CARBS   **221 CALS**

Weight: 233g

60g CARBS   **266 CALS**

Weight: 280g

Tiramisu

15g CARBS   **110 CALS**

Weight: 45g

30g CARBS   **221 CALS**

Weight: 90g

45g CARBS   **328 CALS**

Weight: 134g

60g CARBS   **436 CALS**

Weight: 178g

75g CARBS   **544 CALS**

Weight: 222g

90g CARBS   **649 CALS**

Weight: 265g

Trifle

15g CARBS **193 CALS**

Weight: 55g

30g CARBS **378 CALS**

Weight: 108g

45g CARBS **567 CALS**

Weight: 162g

60g CARBS **753 CALS**

Weight: 215g

75g CARBS **945 CALS**

Weight: 270g

90g CARBS **1138 CALS**

Weight: 325g

Apple Juice

16g CARBS	28g CARBS	57g CARBS
61 CALS	109 CALS	218 CALS

160ml	287ml (half pint)	574ml (pint)

Cranberry Juice

23g CARBS	41g CARBS	83g CARBS
98 CALS	175 CALS	350 CALS

160ml	287ml (half pint)	574ml (pint)

Grapefruit Juice

13g CARBS	24g CARBS	48g CARBS
53 CALS	95 CALS	189 CALS

| 160ml | 287ml (half pint) | 574ml (pint) |

Orange Juice

14g CARBS	25g CARBS	51g CARBS
58 CALS	103 CALS	207 CALS

| 160ml | 287ml (half pint) | 574ml (pint) |

Pineapple Juice

17g CARBS	30g CARBS	60g CARBS
66 CALS	118 CALS	235 CALS

160ml	287ml (half pint)	574ml (pint)

Tomato Juice

5g CARBS	9g CARBS	17g CARBS
22 CALS	40 CALS	80 CALS

160ml	287ml (half pint)	574ml (pint)

Cola

17g CARBS	31g CARBS	63g CARBS
66 CALS	118 CALS	235 CALS

160ml	287ml (half pint)	574ml (pint)

Lucozade Energy

10g CARBS	20g CARBS	30g CARBS
39 CALS	80 CALS	119 CALS

56ml	114ml	170ml

Milk (skimmed)

7g CARBS	13g CARBS	25g CARBS
51 CALS	92 CALS	184 CALS

160ml	287ml (half pint)	574ml (pint)

Milk (semi-skimmed)

8g CARBS	13g CARBS	27g CARBS
74 CALS	132 CALS	264 CALS

160ml	287ml (half pint)	574ml (pint)

Milk (whole)

7g CARBS	13g CARBS	26g CARBS
106 CALS	189 CALS	379 CALS

160ml	287ml (half pint)	574ml (pint)

Soya Milk (sweetened)

4g CARBS	7g CARBS	14g CARBS
69 CALS	123 CALS	247 CALS

160ml	287ml (half pint)	574ml (pint)

Fruit Smoothie (strawberry & banana)

| **20**g CARBS | **84** CALS | **73**g CARBS | **302** CALS |

160ml

574ml (pint)

Milkshake (made with powder & semi-skimmed milk)

| **32**g CARBS | **198** CALS | **65**g CARBS | **396** CALS |

287ml (half pint)

574ml (pint)

Hot Chocolate

28g CARBS   **190** CALS

260ml

Hot Malt Drink

34g CARBS   **221** CALS

260ml

Lager (draught)

| 4g CARBS | 95 CALS | 8g CARBS | 189 CALS |

287ml (half pint)   574ml (pint)

Ale

| 9g CARBS | 86 CALS | 17g CARBS | 172 CALS |

287ml (half pint)   574ml (pint)

Stout

| 4g CARBS | 86 CALS | 9g CARBS | 172 CALS |

287ml (half pint)   574ml (pint)

Cider (dry)

7g CARBS **103** CALS

287ml (half pint)

15g CARBS **207** CALS

574ml (pint)

Cider (sweet)

12g CARBS **121** CALS

287ml (half pint)

25g CARBS **241** CALS

574ml (pint)

Cider (vintage)

21g CARBS **290** CALS

287ml (half pint)

42g CARBS **580** CALS

574ml (pint)

Sweet White Wine

7g CARBS	**118** CALS	**15g** CARBS	**235** CALS

125ml (small glass)

250ml (large glass)

Advocaat

14g CARBS	**136** CALS

50ml

Vermouth (sweet)

8g CARBS	**76** CALS

50ml

Port

6g CARBS	**79** CALS

50ml

Sweet Liqueur

8g CARBS	**64** CALS

25ml

WKD

35g CARBS	207 CALS

	CARBS	CALS
2x	70g	414
3x	105g	621
4x	140g	828
275ml bottle		

WKD Core (cider)

47g CARBS	325 CALS

	CARBS	CALS
2x	94g	650
3x	141g	975
4x	188g	1300
500ml bottle		

Energy Drink

13g CARBS	27g CARBS
55 CALS	111 CALS

125ml (half can)	250ml (full can)

Apricot (fresh)

4g CARBS   **17** CALS

Weight: 55g

8g CARBS   **34** CALS

Weight: 110g

12g CARBS   **51** CALS

Weight: 165g

Apricot (dried)

10g CARBS   **44** CALS

Weight: 28g

20g CARBS   **87** CALS

Weight: 55g

30g CARBS   **130** CALS

Weight: 82g

Apple

10g CARBS   **40 CALS**

Weight: 85g

Blueberries

5g CARBS   **21 CALS**

Weight: 40g

15g CARBS   **62 CALS**

Weight: 131g

15g CARBS   **68 CALS**

Weight: 130g

20g CARBS   **80 CALS**

Weight: 170g

25g CARBS   **112 CALS**

Weight: 215g

Banana

15g CARBS   **60 CALS**

Weight: 63g (without skin)

15g CARBS   **60 CALS**

Weight: 97g (with skin)

20g CARBS   **81 CALS**

Weight: 85g (without skin)

20g CARBS   **81 CALS**

Weight: 130g (with skin)

30g CARBS   **122 CALS**

Weight: 128g (without skin)

30g CARBS   **122 CALS**

Weight: 190g (with skin)

Cherries

5g CARBS   **20** CALS

Weight: 50g (with stones)

Clementine

5g CARBS   **22** CALS

Weight: 80g

10g CARBS   **39** CALS

Weight: 100g (with stones)

10g CARBS   **45** CALS

Weight: 160g

15g CARBS   **62** CALS

Weight: 160g (with stones)

Satsuma

5g CARBS   **22** CALS

Weight: 85g

Fruit Cocktail (in juice)

5g CARBS   **22** CALS

Weight: 75g

15g CARBS   **61** CALS

Weight: 210g (half tin)

30g CARBS   **122** CALS

Weight: 420g (full tin)

Grapefruit

5g CARBS   **24** CALS

Weight: 119g (half)

10g CARBS   **46** CALS

Weight: 228g (whole)

10g CARBS   **46** CALS

Weight: 140g (whole)

Grapes (seedless)

10g CARBS   **39 CALS**

Weight: 65g

20g CARBS   **78 CALS**

Weight: 130g

30g CARBS   **117 CALS**

Weight: 195g

40g CARBS   **156 CALS**

Weight: 260g

50g CARBS   **195 CALS**

Weight: 325g

60g CARBS   **234 CALS**

Weight: 390g

Kiwi

5g CARBS   **24** CALS

Weight: 55g (1 kiwi with skin)

5g CARBS   **24** CALS

Weight: 51g (1 kiwi)

10g CARBS   **47** CALS

Weight: 95g (2 kiwis)

Mango

10g CARBS   **40** CALS

Weight: 70g

20g CARBS   **80** CALS

Weight: 140g

30g CARBS   **120** CALS

Weight: 210g

Melon (honeydew)

10g CARBS	42 CALS

Weight: 150g

20g CARBS	84 CALS

Weight: 300g

30g CARBS	126 CALS

Weight: 450g

Watermelon

10g CARBS	43 CALS

Weight: 140g

20g CARBS	87 CALS

Weight: 280g

30g CARBS	130 CALS

Weight: 420g

Orange

4g CARBS | **18** CALS

Weight: 71g

Papaya

5g CARBS | **24** CALS

Weight: 90g

7g CARBS | **30** CALS

Weight: 115g

10g CARBS | **49** CALS

Weight: 180g

10g CARBS | **45** CALS

Weight: 172g

15g CARBS | **73** CALS

Weight: 270g

Peach (fresh)

5g CARBS | **23 CALS**

Weight: 70g (without stone)

Peach (tinned in juice)

10g CARBS | **39 CALS**

Weight: 100g

10g CARBS | **46 CALS**

Weight: 138g

20g CARBS | **80 CALS**

Weight: 205g (half tin)

15g CARBS | **66 CALS**

Weight: 200g

40g CARBS | **160 CALS**

Weight: 410g (full tin)

Pear

10g CARBS   **42 CALS**

Weight: 104g

Pear (tinned in juice)

10g CARBS   **38 CALS**

Weight: 115g

20g CARBS   **78 CALS**

Weight: 195g

20g CARBS   **76 CALS**

Weight: 230g

30g CARBS   **118 CALS**

Weight: 295g

30g CARBS   **117 CALS**

Weight: 355g (full tin)

Pineapple (fresh)

4g CARBS	**16** CALS

Weight: 40g

8g CARBS	**33** CALS

Weight: 80g

12g CARBS	**49** CALS

Weight: 120g

16g CARBS	**66** CALS

Weight: 160g

20g CARBS	**82** CALS

Weight: 200g

24g CARBS	**98** CALS

Weight: 240g

Pineapple (tinned in juice)

5g CARBS **19 CALS**

Weight: 40g

10g CARBS **38 CALS**

Weight: 80g

20g CARBS **75 CALS**

Weight: 160g

30g CARBS **115 CALS**

Weight: 245g

40g CARBS **155 CALS**

Weight: 330g

50g CARBS **193 CALS**

Weight: 410g (full tin)

Pomegranate

5g CARBS	20 CALS

Weight: 40g

10g CARBS	43 CALS

Weight: 85g

15g CARBS	64 CALS

Weight: 125g

Prune

10g CARBS	42 CALS

Weight: 30g

20g CARBS	85 CALS

Weight: 60g

30g CARBS	125 CALS

Weight: 89g

Plum

| **5g** CARBS | **20** CALS | | **10g** CARBS | **40** CALS |

CARBS	CALS
10g	40
15g	60
20g	80
Weight: 55g	

	CARBS	CALS
2x	20g	80
3x	30g	120
4x	40g	160
Weight: 110g		

Nectarine

| **7g** CARBS | **32** CALS | | **15g** CARBS | **66** CALS |

CARBS	CALS
14g	64
21g	96
28g	128
Weight: 80g (without stone)	

	CARBS	CALS
2x	30g	132
3x	45g	198
4x	60g	264
Weight: 165g		

Raspberries

5g CARBS   **26** CALS

Weight: 105g

Strawberries

5g CARBS   **23** CALS

Weight: 85g

10g CARBS   **53** CALS

Weight: 210g

15g CARBS   **68** CALS

Weight: 250g

15g CARBS   **80** CALS

Weight: 320g

25g CARBS   **111** CALS

Weight: 410g

Raisins

10g CARBS | **41** CALS

Weight: 15g

20g CARBS | **79** CALS

Weight: 29g

30g CARBS | **120** CALS

Weight: 44g

Sultanas

10g CARBS | **41** CALS

Weight: 15g

20g CARBS | **80** CALS

Weight: 29g

30g CARBS | **118** CALS

Weight: 43g

Beans on Toast (with margarine)

22g CARBS   **151** CALS

Weight: 92g

32g CARBS   **205** CALS

Weight: 157g

42g CARBS   **260** CALS

Weight: 222g

55g CARBS   **356** CALS

Weight: 249g (half tin of beans)

70g CARBS   **438** CALS

Weight: 347g

85g CARBS   **520** CALS

Weight: 444g (full tin of beans)

Chicken Goujons, Potato Faces & Peas

18g CARBS	172 CALS

Weight: 89g

38g CARBS	346 CALS

Weight: 178g

56g CARBS	518 CALS

Weight: 267g

76g CARBS	691 CALS

Weight: 356g

93g CARBS	864 CALS

Weight: 445g

113g CARBS	1038 CALS

Weight: 534g

Chilli con Carne with White Rice

15g CARBS **137** CALS

Weight: 122g

40g CARBS **307** CALS

Weight: 266g

65g CARBS **483** CALS

Weight: 413g

91g CARBS **661** CALS

Weight: 565g

116g CARBS **843** CALS

Weight: 720g

141g CARBS **1015** CALS

Weight: 865g

Corned Beef Hash

12g CARBS	141 CALS

Weight: 100g

25g CARBS	282 CALS

Weight: 200g

37g CARBS	423 CALS

Weight: 300g

49g CARBS	564 CALS

Weight: 400g

62g CARBS	705 CALS

Weight: 500g

74g CARBS	846 CALS

Weight: 600g

Curry (chicken) with White Rice

12g CARBS   **146** CALS

Weight: 136g

35g CARBS   **390** CALS

Weight: 358g

57g CARBS   **580** CALS

Weight: 526g

79g CARBS   **810** CALS

Weight: 733g

101g CARBS   **1013** CALS

Weight: 915g

124g CARBS   **1267** CALS

Weight: 1147g

Curry (lentil) with Brown Rice

20g CARBS   **178 CALS**

Weight: 125g

50g CARBS   **399 CALS**

Weight: 280g

80g CARBS   **621 CALS**

Weight: 437g

110g CARBS   **852 CALS**

Weight: 599g

140g CARBS   **1075 CALS**

Weight: 756g

170g CARBS   **1300 CALS**

Weight: 914g

Curry (veg & potato) with White Rice

20g CARBS   **120 CALS**

Weight: 122g

49g CARBS   **281 CALS**

Weight: 272g

78g CARBS   **443 CALS**

Weight: 423g

108g CARBS   **607 CALS**

Weight: 577g

138g CARBS   **772 CALS**

Weight: 731g

167g CARBS   **935 CALS**

Weight: 885g

Fish Fingers, Oven Chips & Beans

30g CARBS	185 CALS

Weight: 131g

51g CARBS	316 CALS

Weight: 229g

70g CARBS	444 CALS

Weight: 325g

90g CARBS	578 CALS

Weight: 425g

111g CARBS	714 CALS

Weight: 528g

131g CARBS	844 CALS

Weight: 625g

Fish Pie

11g CARBS **148** CALS	**22**g CARBS **295** CALS

Weight: 125g	Weight: 250g

34g CARBS **448** CALS	**45**g CARBS **596** CALS

Weight: 380g	Weight: 505g

56g CARBS **743** CALS	**68**g CARBS **897** CALS

Weight: 630g	Weight: 760g

Lasagne

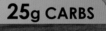

10g CARBS   **146 CALS**

Weight: 80g

25g CARBS   **357 CALS**

Weight: 195g

40g CARBS   **576 CALS**

Weight: 315g

55g CARBS   **787 CALS**

Weight: 430g

70g CARBS   **997 CALS**

Weight: 545g

85g CARBS   **1217 CALS**

Weight: 665g

Macaroni Cheese

14g CARBS   **166 CALS**

Weight: 80g

30g CARBS   **337 CALS**

Weight: 163g

40g CARBS   **460 CALS**

Weight: 222g

55g CARBS   **629 CALS**

Weight: 304g

70g CARBS   **797 CALS**

Weight: 385g

84g CARBS   **963 CALS**

Weight: 465g

Enchilada

32g CARBS   **318 CALS**

	CARBS	CALS
2x	64g	636
3x	96g	954
4x	128g	1272

Weight: 146g

Fajita

30g CARBS   **245 CALS**

	CARBS	CALS
2x	60g	490
3x	90g	735
4x	120g	980

Weight: 160g

Quesadilla

18g CARBS   **159 CALS**

	CARBS	CALS
2x	36g	318
3x	54g	477
4x	72g	636

Weight: 74g

Taco

11g CARBS   **219 CALS**

	CARBS	CALS
2x	22g	438
3x	33g	657
4x	44g	876

Weight: 80g

Pasta Bake

15g CARBS   **108 CALS**

Weight: 70g

30g CARBS   **220 CALS**

Weight: 143g

45g CARBS   **330 CALS**

Weight: 214g

60g CARBS   **439 CALS**

Weight: 285g

75g CARBS   **547 CALS**

Weight: 355g

90g CARBS   **656 CALS**

Weight: 426g

Pasta Meal (chicken & broccoli)

10g CARBS   110 CALS

Weight: 65g

25g CARBS   281 CALS

Weight: 166g

40g CARBS   451 CALS

Weight: 267g

51g CARBS   576 CALS

Weight: 341g

67g CARBS   747 CALS

Weight: 442g

82g CARBS   918 CALS

Weight: 543g

Chicken & Bacon Pie

50g CARBS | **702 CALS**

Weight: 264g

Steak Pie

56g CARBS | **632 CALS**

Weight: 244g

Steak & Kidney Pudding

34g CARBS | **382 CALS**

Weight: 182g

Top Crust Pie

25g CARBS | **362 CALS**

Weight: 264g

Steak & Potato Pie

25g CARBS | **307 CALS**

Weight: 130g

50g CARBS | **625 CALS**

Weight: 265g

Pizza (chicken, deep pan - oven baked)

20g CARBS   143 CALS

	CARBS	CALS
2x	40g	286
3x	60g	429
4x	80g	572
Weight: 65g		

40g CARBS   286 CALS

	CARBS	CALS
2x	80g	572
3x	120g	858
4x	160g	1144
Weight: 130g		

61g CARBS   429 CALS

	CARBS	CALS
2x	122g	858
3x	183g	1287
4x	244g	1716
Weight: 195g		

80g CARBS   568 CALS

	CARBS	CALS
2x	160g	1136
3x	240g	1704
4x	320g	2272
Weight: 258g		

Pizza (pepperoni, thin crust - oven baked)

11g CARBS   102 CALS

	CARBS	CALS
2x	22g	204
3x	33g	306
4x	44g	408
Weight: 40g		

20g CARBS   191 CALS

	CARBS	CALS
2x	40g	382
3x	60g	573
4x	80g	764
Weight: 75g		

30g CARBS   293 CALS

	CARBS	CALS
2x	60g	586
3x	90g	879
4x	120g	1172
Weight: 115g		

41g CARBS   395 CALS

	CARBS	CALS
2x	82g	790
3x	123g	1185
4x	164g	1580
Weight: 155g		

Quiche Lorraine, Salad & Coleslaw

16g CARBS	**410 CALS**

Weight: 145g

29g CARBS	**668 CALS**

Weight: 215g

44g CARBS	**1074 CALS**

Weight: 340g

57g CARBS	**1314 CALS**

Weight: 405g

73g CARBS	**1722 CALS**

Weight: 535g

86g CARBS	**1980 CALS**

Weight: 605g

Risotto

20g CARBS   **169 CALS**

Weight: 120g

40g CARBS   **340 CALS**

Weight: 241g

60g CARBS   **512 CALS**

Weight: 363g

80g CARBS   **684 CALS**

Weight: 485g

100g CARBS   **856 CALS**

Weight: 607g

120g CARBS   **1028 CALS**

Weight: 729g

Sausage, Mash (with butter) & Onion Gravy

25g CARBS	297 CALS

Weight: 200g

49g CARBS	587 CALS

Weight: 395g

73g CARBS	883 CALS

Weight: 595g

98g CARBS	1175 CALS

Weight: 790g

122g CARBS	1472 CALS

Weight: 990g

146g CARBS	1762 CALS

Weight: 1185g

Shepherd's Pie

12g CARBS   175 CALS

Weight: 120g

25g CARBS   350 CALS

Weight: 240g

37g CARBS   526 CALS

Weight: 360g

50g CARBS   708 CALS

Weight: 485g

63g CARBS   883 CALS

Weight: 605g

76g CARBS   1066 CALS

Weight: 730g

Chicken Noodle Soup

5g CARBS	26 CALS

Weight: 130g

10g CARBS	52 CALS

Weight: 260g

15g CARBS	80 CALS

Weight: 400g

Chunky Veg Soup

10g CARBS	57 CALS

Weight: 133g

20g CARBS	114 CALS

Weight: 266g

30g CARBS	172 CALS

Weight: 400g (full tin)

Mushroom Soup

5g CARBS | **69 CALS**

Weight: 130g

Tomato Soup

10g CARBS | **84 CALS**

Weight: 135g

10g CARBS | **138 CALS**

Weight: 260g

20g CARBS | **171 CALS**

Weight: 275g

15g CARBS | **207 CALS**

Weight: 390g (full tin)

30g CARBS | **254 CALS**

Weight: 410g (full tin)

Spaghetti Bolognaise

15g CARBS   **144 CALS**

Weight: 153g

40g CARBS   **334 CALS**

Weight: 335g

65g CARBS   **527 CALS**

Weight: 518g

90g CARBS   **720 CALS**

Weight: 703g

115g CARBS   **915 CALS**

Weight: 891g

140g CARBS   **1114 CALS**

Weight: 1084g

Stew & Dumplings

20g CARBS **204 CALS**

Weight: 140g

40g CARBS **397 CALS**

Weight: 265g

65g CARBS **658 CALS**

Weight: 490g

85g CARBS **855 CALS**

Weight: 620g

105g CARBS **1062 CALS**

Weight: 765g

125g CARBS **1259 CALS**

Weight: 895g

Stir-fry (chicken)

10g CARBS   81 CALS

Weight: 70g

21g CARBS   162 CALS

Weight: 140g

30g CARBS   238 CALS

Weight: 205g

41g CARBS   319 CALS

Weight: 275g

51g CARBS   400 CALS

Weight: 345g

61g CARBS   477 CALS

Weight: 411g

Sushi

8g CARBS   56 CALS

	CARBS	CALS
2x	16g	112
3x	24g	168
4x	32g	224
Weight: 34g		

14g CARBS   114 CALS

	CARBS	CALS
2x	28g	228
3x	42g	342
4x	56g	456
Weight: 36g		

7g CARBS   62 CALS

	CARBS	CALS
2x	14g	124
3x	21g	186
4x	28g	248
Weight: 28g		

5g CARBS   64 CALS

	CARBS	CALS
2x	10g	128
3x	15g	192
4x	20g	256
Weight: 24g		

Toad in the Hole

20g CARBS	**269** CALS

Weight: 92g

40g CARBS	**534** CALS

Weight: 183g

60g CARBS	**803** CALS

Weight: 275g

80g CARBS	**1069** CALS

Weight: 366g

100g CARBS	**1335** CALS

Weight: 457g

119g CARBS	**1603** CALS

Weight: 549g

Coleslaw

| 5g CARBS | 103 CALS | 10g CARBS | 207 CALS |

Weight: 65g

Weight: 130g

Onion Rings

| 10g CARBS | 78 CALS | 20g CARBS | 156 CALS |

Weight: 26g

Weight: 52g

Potato Salad (with mayonnaise)

| 10g CARBS | 198 CALS | 20g CARBS | 397 CALS |

Weight: 83g

Weight: 166g

Stuffing

20g CARBS	99 CALS

Weight: 65g

40g CARBS	198 CALS

Weight: 130g

60g CARBS	296 CALS

Weight: 195g

Yorkshire Pudding

10g CARBS	84 CALS

Weight: 40g

20g CARBS	168 CALS

Weight: 80g

30g CARBS	252 CALS

Weight: 120g

Apple Chutney

10g CARBS   **38 CALS**

Weight: 20g

Brown Sauce

5g CARBS   **21 CALS**

Weight: 21g

Cranberry Sauce

5g CARBS   **22 CALS**

Weight: 14g

Horseradish

5g CARBS   **40 CALS**

Weight: 26g

Ketchup

5g CARBS   **22 CALS**

Weight: 19g

Mint Sauce

5g CARBS   **21 CALS**

Weight: 21g

Piccalilli

5g CARBS | **24** CALS

Weight: 22g

Pickle

10g CARBS | **39** CALS

Weight: 28g

Salad Cream

5g CARBS | **94** CALS

Weight: 27g

Sweet Chilli Sauce

5g CARBS | **20** CALS

Weight: 10g

Tartar Sauce

5g CARBS | **78** CALS

Weight: 26g

Thousand Island

5g CARBS | **116** CALS

Weight: 36g

Fish (battered)

9g CARBS   **137 CALS**

Weight: 65g

19g CARBS   **274 CALS**

Weight: 130g

38g CARBS   **559 CALS**

Weight: 265g

Fish (breaded)

8g CARBS   **121 CALS**

Weight: 53g

16g CARBS   **243 CALS**

Weight: 106g

24g CARBS   **357 CALS**

Weight: 156g

Fish Cake

| 8g CARBS | 98 CALS | | 14g CARBS | 169 CALS |

	CARBS	CALS
2x	16g	196
3x	24g	294
4x	32g	392
Weight: 52g		

	CARBS	CALS
2x	28g	338
3x	42g	507
4x	56g	676
Weight: 90g		

Fish Finger

| 3g CARBS | 40 CALS |

Fish Goujon

| 5g CARBS | 64 CALS |

	CARBS	CALS
2x	6g	80
3x	9g	120
4x	12g	160
Weight: 20g		

	CARBS	CALS
2x	10g	128
3x	15g	192
4x	20g	256
Weight: 30g		

Scampi

20g CARBS   **221** CALS

Weight: 70g

40g CARBS   **442** CALS

Weight: 140g

60g CARBS   **657** CALS

Weight: 208g

Haggis

20g CARBS   **326** CALS

Weight: 105g

40g CARBS   **651** CALS

Weight: 210g

60g CARBS   **977** CALS

Weight: 315g

Black Pudding

11g CARBS   **146 CALS**

	CARBS	CALS
2x	22g	292
3x	33g	438
4x	44g	584
Weight: 58g		

Chicken Goujon

6g CARBS   **83 CALS**

	CARBS	CALS
2x	12g	166
3x	18g	249
4x	24g	332
Weight: 30g		

Sausage (thin)

2g CARBS   **59 CALS**

	CARBS	CALS
2x	4g	118
3x	6g	177
4x	8g	236
Weight: 20g		

Sausage (thick)

5g CARBS   **162 CALS**

	CARBS	CALS
2x	10g	324
3x	15g	486
4x	20g	648
Weight: 55g		

Chicken Kiev

| 15g CARBS | 348 CALS | 30g CARBS | 697 CALS |

Weight: 130g

Weight: 260g

Pork Pie

| 30g CARBS | 447 CALS | 80g CARBS | 1203 CALS |

Weight: 119g

Weight: 320g

Scotch Egg

| 8g CARBS | 151 CALS | 16g CARBS | 301 CALS |

Weight: 60g

Weight: 120g

Cornish Pasty

10g CARBS   **103** CALS

Weight: 31g

50g CARBS   **538** CALS

Weight: 162g

60g CARBS   **644** CALS

Weight: 194g

135g CARBS   **1441** CALS

Weight: 434g

Sausage Roll

16g CARBS   **241** CALS

Weight: 63g

31g CARBS   **475** CALS

Weight: 124g

Sausages & Beans (tinned)

10g CARBS   **76 CALS**

Weight: 70g

20g CARBS   **152 CALS**

Weight: 140g

30g CARBS   **228 CALS**

Weight: 210g (half tin)

40g CARBS   **310 CALS**

Weight: 285g

50g CARBS   **386 CALS**

Weight: 355g

60g CARBS   **462 CALS**

Weight: 425g (full tin)

Cassava Chips

30g CARBS **159 CALS**

Weight: 45g

60g CARBS **321 CALS**

Weight: 91g

90g CARBS **480 CALS**

Weight: 136g

120g CARBS **642 CALS**

Weight: 182g

150g CARBS **805 CALS**

Weight: 228g

180g CARBS **960 CALS**

Weight: 272g

Chips (deep fried)

10g CARBS	79 CALS

Weight: 33g

30g CARBS	237 CALS

Weight: 99g

50g CARBS	394 CALS

Weight: 165g

70g CARBS	550 CALS

Weight: 230g

90g CARBS	705 CALS

Weight: 295g

110g CARBS	860 CALS

Weight: 360g

Chips (oven)

10g CARBS	53 CALS

Weight: 33g

30g CARBS	162 CALS

Weight: 100g

50g CARBS	272 CALS

Weight: 168g

70g CARBS	381 CALS

Weight: 235g

90g CARBS	491 CALS

Weight: 303g

110g CARBS	599 CALS

Weight: 370g

Dauphinoise Potatoes

10g CARBS   **178 CALS**

Weight: 72g

20g CARBS   **363 CALS**

Weight: 147g

30g CARBS   **548 CALS**

Weight: 222g

40g CARBS   **734 CALS**

Weight: 297g

50g CARBS   **921 CALS**

Weight: 373g

60g CARBS   **1107 CALS**

Weight: 448g

Gnocchi

30g CARBS **136 CALS**

Weight: 80g

60g CARBS **272 CALS**

Weight: 160g

90g CARBS **408 CALS**

Weight: 240g

120g CARBS **547 CALS**

Weight: 322g

150g CARBS **683 CALS**

Weight: 402g

180g CARBS **819 CALS**

Weight: 482g

Jacket Potato (with skin)

20g CARBS	95 CALS

Weight: 95g

35g CARBS	160 CALS

Weight: 158g

45g CARBS	211 CALS

Weight: 220g

60g CARBS	280 CALS

Weight: 284g

75g CARBS	351 CALS

Weight: 348g

90g CARBS	407 CALS

Weight: 410g

Mashed Potato (with butter)

19g CARBS   **125 CALS**

Weight: 120g

36g CARBS   **244 CALS**

Weight: 235g

55g CARBS   **369 CALS**

Weight: 355g

73g CARBS   **489 CALS**

Weight: 470g

91g CARBS   **614 CALS**

Weight: 590g

109g CARBS   **733 CALS**

Weight: 705g

New Potatoes

10g CARBS   **43 CALS**

Weight: 65g

20g CARBS   **86 CALS**

Weight: 130g

30g CARBS   **129 CALS**

Weight: 195g

40g CARBS   **172 CALS**

Weight: 260g

60g CARBS   **257 CALS**

Weight: 390g

80g CARBS   **343 CALS**

Weight: 520g

Potato Faces

10g CARBS	72 CALS

Weight: 34g

21g CARBS	145 CALS

Weight: 68g

31g CARBS	217 CALS

Weight: 102g

42g CARBS	290 CALS

Weight: 136g

52g CARBS	362 CALS

Weight: 170g

63g CARBS	435 CALS

Weight: 204g

Roast Potatoes

10g CARBS   **57 CALS**

Weight: 38g

25g CARBS   **142 CALS**

Weight: 95g

40g CARBS   **231 CALS**

Weight: 155g

55g CARBS   **316 CALS**

Weight: 212g

70g CARBS   **402 CALS**

Weight: 270g

85g CARBS   **492 CALS**

Weight: 330g

Sauté Potatoes (baked)

10g CARBS   **62 CALS**

Weight: 28g

20g CARBS   **121 CALS**

Weight: 55g

30g CARBS   **176 CALS**

Weight: 80g

40g CARBS   **238 CALS**

Weight: 108g

50g CARBS   **297 CALS**

Weight: 135g

60g CARBS   **356 CALS**

Weight: 162g

Sweet Potatoes (baked)

15g CARBS   **63 CALS**

Weight: 55g

30g CARBS   **124 CALS**

Weight: 108g

45g CARBS   **184 CALS**

Weight: 160g

60g CARBS   **247 CALS**

Weight: 215g

75g CARBS   **311 CALS**

Weight: 270g

90g CARBS   **370 CALS**

Weight: 322g

Wedges

10g CARBS   68 CALS

Weight: 55g

20g CARBS   135 CALS

Weight: 110g

30g CARBS   203 CALS

Weight: 165g

40g CARBS   271 CALS

Weight: 220g

50g CARBS   332 CALS

Weight: 270g

60g CARBS   400 CALS

Weight: 325g

Hash Brown

10g CARBS   **88** CALS

	CARBS	CALS
2x	20g	176
3x	30g	264
4x	40g	352
Weight: 44g		

Potato Croquette

5g CARBS   **47** CALS

	CARBS	CALS
2x	10g	94
3x	15g	141
4x	20g	188
Weight: 22g		

Potato Rosti

20g CARBS   **155** CALS

	CARBS	CALS
2x	40g	310
3x	60g	465
4x	80g	620
Weight: 80g		

Potato Waffle

15g CARBS   **98** CALS

	CARBS	CALS
2x	30g	196
3x	45g	294
4x	60g	392
Weight: 49g		

Bulgar Wheat

20g CARBS   **94** CALS

Weight: 100g

40g CARBS   **188** CALS

Weight: 200g

60g CARBS   **277** CALS

Weight: 295g

Quinoa

20g CARBS   **109** CALS

Weight: 85g

40g CARBS   **220** CALS

Weight: 172g

60g CARBS   **333** CALS

Weight: 260g

Couscous

10g CARBS   **50 CALS**

Weight: 45g

25g CARBS   **121 CALS**

Weight: 110g

40g CARBS   **193 CALS**

Weight: 175g

55g CARBS   **264 CALS**

Weight: 240g

70g CARBS   **336 CALS**

Weight: 305g

85g CARBS   **407 CALS**

Weight: 370g

Noodles (egg)

20g CARBS   **101 CALS**

Weight: 58g

40g CARBS   **200 CALS**

Weight: 115g

60g CARBS   **296 CALS**

Weight: 170g

80g CARBS   **397 CALS**

Weight: 228g

100g CARBS   **496 CALS**

Weight: 285g

120g CARBS   **595 CALS**

Weight: 342g

Noodles (rice)

20g CARBS   **86 CALS**

Weight: 70g

40g CARBS   **175 CALS**

Weight: 142g

60g CARBS   **264 CALS**

Weight: 215g

80g CARBS   **351 CALS**

Weight: 285g

100g CARBS   **440 CALS**

Weight: 358g

120g CARBS   **529 CALS**

Weight: 430g

Pasta (bows)

10g CARBS	50 CALS

Weight: 30g

30g CARBS	148 CALS

Weight: 88g

50g CARBS	249 CALS

Weight: 148g

70g CARBS	344 CALS

Weight: 205g

90g CARBS	445 CALS

Weight: 265g

110g CARBS	543 CALS

Weight: 323g

Pasta (macaroni)

10g CARBS   **49 CALS**

Weight: 32g

30g CARBS   **152 CALS**

Weight: 100g

50g CARBS   **252 CALS**

Weight: 166g

70g CARBS   **354 CALS**

Weight: 233g

90g CARBS   **456 CALS**

Weight: 300g

110g CARBS   **556 CALS**

Weight: 366g

Pasta (penne)

10g CARBS	50 CALS	30g CARBS	150 CALS

Weight: 30g   Weight: 90g

50g CARBS	247 CALS	70g CARBS	347 CALS

Weight: 148g   Weight: 208g

90g CARBS	443 CALS	110g CARBS	543 CALS

Weight: 265g   Weight: 325g

Pasta (shells)

10g CARBS	50 CALS

Weight: 30g

30g CARBS	147 CALS

Weight: 88g

50g CARBS	247 CALS

Weight: 148g

70g CARBS	342 CALS

Weight: 205g

90g CARBS	443 CALS

Weight: 265g

110g CARBS	539 CALS

Weight: 323g

Pasta (tagliatelle)

10g CARBS	**53** CALS

Weight: 30g

30g CARBS	**158** CALS

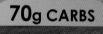

Weight: 90g

50g CARBS	**263** CALS

Weight: 150g

70g CARBS	**368** CALS

Weight: 210g

90g CARBS	**473** CALS

Weight: 270g

110g CARBS	**578** CALS

Weight: 330g

Pasta (twirls)

10g CARBS   **50 CALS**

Weight: 30g

30g CARBS   **148 CALS**

Weight: 88g

50g CARBS   **249 CALS**

Weight: 148g

70g CARBS   **344 CALS**

Weight: 205g

90g CARBS   **445 CALS**

Weight: 265g

110g CARBS   **543 CALS**

Weight: 323g

Pasta (twists)

10g CARBS	51 CALS

Weight: 30g

30g CARBS	149 CALS

Weight: 88g

50g CARBS	245 CALS

Weight: 145g

70g CARBS	343 CALS

Weight: 203g

90g CARBS	439 CALS

Weight: 260g

110g CARBS	537 CALS

Weight: 318g

Pasta (vermicelli)

10g CARBS   **52 CALS**

Weight: 40g

30g CARBS   **161 CALS**

Weight: 125g

50g CARBS   **271 CALS**

Weight: 210g

70g CARBS   **374 CALS**

Weight: 290g

90g CARBS   **484 CALS**

Weight: 375g

110g CARBS   **593 CALS**

Weight: 460g

Rice (white)

10g CARBS	44 CALS

Weight: 32g

30g CARBS	132 CALS

Weight: 96g

50g CARBS	225 CALS

Weight: 163g

70g CARBS	311 CALS

Weight: 225g

90g CARBS	400 CALS

Weight: 290g

110g CARBS	490 CALS

Weight: 355g

Rice (brown)

10g CARBS   **42 CALS**

Weight: 30g

30g CARBS   **134 CALS**

Weight: 95g

50g CARBS   **219 CALS**

Weight: 155g

70g CARBS   **307 CALS**

Weight: 218g

90g CARBS   **395 CALS**

Weight: 280g

110g CARBS   **484 CALS**

Weight: 343g

Rice (sticky white)

20g CARBS **104 CALS**

Weight: 80g

Polenta

10g CARBS **47 CALS**

Weight: 65g

40g CARBS **202 CALS**

Weight: 155g

20g CARBS **93 CALS**

Weight: 130g

60g CARBS **306 CALS**

Weight: 235g

30g CARBS **137 CALS**

Weight: 190g

Ravioli (fresh, meat-filled)

10g CARBS	70 CALS

Weight: 40g

30g CARBS	200 CALS

Weight: 115g

50g CARBS	334 CALS

Weight: 192g

70g CARBS	470 CALS

Weight: 270g

90g CARBS	600 CALS

Weight: 345g

110g CARBS	734 CALS

Weight: 422g

Spaghetti (white)

10g CARBS **52 CALS**

Weight: 33g

30g CARBS **149 CALS**

Weight: 95g

50g CARBS **248 CALS**

Weight: 158g

70g CARBS **345 CALS**

Weight: 220g

90g CARBS **447 CALS**

Weight: 285g

110g CARBS **546 CALS**

Weight: 348g

Spaghetti (wholemeal)

10g CARBS　**48 CALS**

Weight: 33g

30g CARBS　**151 CALS**

Weight: 105g

50g CARBS　**248 CALS**

Weight: 172g

70g CARBS　**346 CALS**

Weight: 240g

90g CARBS　**446 CALS**

Weight: 310g

110g CARBS　**547 CALS**

Weight: 380g

Tortellini (fresh, cheese-filled)

15g CARBS   **103 CALS**

Weight: 42g

50g CARBS   **348 CALS**

Weight: 142g

85g CARBS   **593 CALS**

Weight: 242g

120g CARBS   **838 CALS**

Weight: 342g

155g CARBS   **1083 CALS**

Weight: 442g

190g CARBS   **1328 CALS**

Weight: 542g

Pasta Shapes (tinned)

9g CARBS   **42 CALS**

Weight: 70g

17g CARBS   **84 CALS**

Weight: 140g

26g CARBS   **126 CALS**

Weight: 210g (half tin)

35g CARBS   **171 CALS**

Weight: 285g

44g CARBS   **213 CALS**

Weight: 355g

52g CARBS   **255 CALS**

Weight: 425g (full tin)

Ravioli in Tomato Sauce (tinned)

7g CARBS   **49 CALS**

Weight: 70g

14g CARBS   **98 CALS**

Weight: 140g

22g CARBS   **147 CALS**

Weight: 210g (half tin)

29g CARBS   **200 CALS**

Weight: 285g

37g CARBS   **249 CALS**

Weight: 355g

44g CARBS   **298 CALS**

Weight: 425g (full tin)

Spaghetti in Tomato Sauce (tinned)

10g CARBS	45 CALS

Weight: 70g

20g CARBS	90 CALS

Weight: 140g

30g CARBS	134 CALS

Weight: 210g (half tin)

40g CARBS	182 CALS

Weight: 285g

50g CARBS	227 CALS

Weight: 355g

60g CARBS	272 CALS

Weight: 425g (full tin)

Spaghetti Hoops in Tomato Sauce (tinned)

9g CARBS	41 CALS

Weight: 70g

17g CARBS	82 CALS

Weight: 140g

26g CARBS	123 CALS

Weight: 210g (half tin)

35g CARBS	163 CALS

Weight: 280g

43g CARBS	204 CALS

Weight: 350g

52g CARBS	245 CALS

Weight: 420g (full tin)

Crisps

10g CARBS   **95 CALS**

Weight: 18g

20g CARBS   **201 CALS**

Weight: 38g

30g CARBS   **297 CALS**

Weight: 56g

40g CARBS   **398 CALS**

Weight: 75g

50g CARBS   **498 CALS**

Weight: 94g

60g CARBS   **594 CALS**

Weight: 112g

Bombay Mix

10g CARBS | **141** CALS

Weight: 28g

20g CARBS | **282** CALS

Weight: 56g

30g CARBS | **428** CALS

Weight: 85g

Cashew Nuts

5g CARBS | **171** CALS

Weight: 28g

10g CARBS | **336** CALS

Weight: 55g

15g CARBS | **489** CALS

Weight: 80g

Dried Fruit & Nuts

10g CARBS | **92 CALS**

Weight: 22g

Peanuts (roasted)

5g CARBS | **421 CALS**

Weight: 70g

20g CARBS | **185 CALS**

Weight: 44g

10g CARBS | **843 CALS**

Weight: 140g

30g CARBS | **277 CALS**

Weight: 66g

15g CARBS | **1264 CALS**

Weight: 210g

Popcorn (plain)

5g CARBS	59 CALS

Weight: 10g

10g CARBS	119 CALS

Weight: 20g

15g CARBS	178 CALS

Weight: 30g

20g CARBS	243 CALS

Weight: 41g

25g CARBS	302 CALS

Weight: 51g

30g CARBS	362 CALS

Weight: 61g

Popcorn (sweet)

17g CARBS	106 CALS

Weight: 22g

35g CARBS	216 CALS

Weight: 45g

53g CARBS	326 CALS

Weight: 68g

70g CARBS	432 CALS

Weight: 90g

88g CARBS	542 CALS

Weight: 113g

105g CARBS	648 CALS

Weight: 135g

Prawn Crackers

5g CARBS   **51 CALS**

Weight: 9g

10g CARBS   **103 CALS**

Weight: 18g

20g CARBS   **200 CALS**

Weight: 35g

30g CARBS   **296 CALS**

Weight: 52g

40g CARBS   **388 CALS**

Weight: 68g

50g CARBS   **490 CALS**

Weight: 86g

Tortilla Chips

10g CARBS   **30** CALS

Weight: 16g

Houmous

5g CARBS   **84** CALS

Weight: 45g

30g CARBS   **230** CALS

Weight: 50g

10g CARBS   **168** CALS

Weight: 90g

60g CARBS   **459** CALS

Weight: 100g

15g CARBS   **243** CALS

Weight: 130g

Pretzels

10g CARBS	49 CALS

Weight: 13g

20g CARBS	99 CALS

Weight: 26g

30g CARBS	152 CALS

Weight: 40g

Fudge

10g CARBS	53 CALS

Weight: 12g

20g CARBS	110 CALS

Weight: 25g

30g CARBS	162 CALS

Weight: 37g

Chocolate (milk)

9g CARBS   **83 CALS**

Weight: 16g

19g CARBS   **172 CALS**

Weight: 33g

28g CARBS   **260 CALS**

Weight: 50g

38g CARBS   **348 CALS**

Weight: 67g

48g CARBS   **442 CALS**

Weight: 85g

57g CARBS   **525 CALS**

Weight: 101g

Chocolate (dark)

10g CARBS	82 CALS

Weight: 16g

20g CARBS	163 CALS

Weight: 32g

30g CARBS	245 CALS

Weight: 48g

40g CARBS	321 CALS

Weight: 63g

50g CARBS	398 CALS

Weight: 78g

60g CARBS	479 CALS

Weight: 94g

Chocolate Mint

10g CARBS   **75 CALS**

	CARBS	CALS
2x	20g	150
3x	30g	225
4x	40g	300
Weight: 15g		

Licorice Allsorts

10g CARBS   **43 CALS**

	CARBS	CALS
2x	20g	86
3x	30g	129
4x	40g	172
Weight: 12g		

Individual Chocolate

7g CARBS   **52 CALS**

	CARBS	CALS
2x	14g	104
3x	21g	156
4x	28g	208
Weight: 11g		

8g CARBS   **76 CALS**

	CARBS	CALS
2x	16g	152
3x	24g	228
4x	32g	304
Weight: 14g		

Cola Bottles

10g CARBS   **46** CALS

	CARBS	CALS
2x	20g	92
3x	30g	138
4x	40g	184
Weight: 13g		

Jelly Babies

12g CARBS   **60** CALS

	CARBS	CALS
2x	24g	120
3x	36g	180
4x	48g	240
Weight: 18g		

Jelly Beans

10g CARBS   **42** CALS

	CARBS	CALS
2x	20g	84
3x	30g	126
4x	40g	168
Weight: 11g		

Wine Gums

10g CARBS   **41** CALS

	CARBS	CALS
2x	20g	82
3x	30g	123
4x	40g	164
Weight: 14g		

Fish Stew with Jollof Rice

40g CARBS   **388** CALS

Weight: 275g

Fufu (yam)

49g CARBS   **202** CALS

Weight: 130g

85g CARBS   **811** CALS

Weight: 575g

99g CARBS   **411** CALS

Weight: 265g

125g CARBS   **1199** CALS

Weight: 850g

140g CARBS   **581** CALS

Weight: 375g

Beef Burger (with cheese)

31g CARBS   **519** CALS

Weight: 181g

French Fries

33g CARBS   **269** CALS

Weight: 96g (small)

Chicken Burger

45g CARBS   **398** CALS

Weight: 168g

54g CARBS   **448** CALS

Weight: 160g (medium)

Veggie Burger

41g CARBS   **321** CALS

Weight: 158g

77g CARBS   **636** CALS

Weight: 227g (large)

Caribbean - Fried Fish, Rice & Peas

56g CARBS   **555 CALS**

Weight: 265g

113g CARBS   **1110 CALS**

Weight: 530g

Caribbean - Goat Curry, Rice & Peas

55g CARBS   **630 CALS**

Weight: 375g

110g CARBS   **1260 CALS**

Weight: 750g

Caribbean - Jerk Chicken, Rice & Peas

49g CARBS   **511 CALS**

Weight: 405g

98g CARBS   **1023 CALS**

Weight: 810g

Caribbean - Jamaican Beef Patty

20g CARBS	206 CALS

Weight: 85g

40g CARBS	407 CALS

Weight: 170g

Caribbean - Rice & Peas

45g CARBS	240 CALS

Weight: 150g (half tray)

91g CARBS	480 CALS

Weight: 300g (full tray)

Chinese - Duck Pancake

5g CARBS	95 CALS

Weight: 50g

5g CARBS	95 CALS

Weight: 50g

Chinese - Chicken Balls

5g CARBS | **97** CALS

Weight: 38g

20g CARBS | **357** CALS

Weight: 140g (half tray)

40g CARBS | **714** CALS

Weight: 280g (full tray)

Chinese - Prawn Toast

5g CARBS | **123** CALS

Weight: 32g

10g CARBS | **234** CALS

Weight: 61g

15g CARBS | **345** CALS

Weight: 90g (full tray)

Chinese - Beef Chow Mein

40g CARBS	**374** CALS

80g CARBS	**741** CALS

Weight: 275g (half tray)   Weight: 545g (full tray)

Chinese - Chicken Curry

5g CARBS	**276** CALS

10g CARBS	**551** CALS

Weight: 190g (half tray)   Weight: 380g (full tray)

Chinese - Singapore Noodles

25g CARBS	**338** CALS

50g CARBS	**677** CALS

Weight: 205g (half tray)   Weight: 410g (full tray)

Chinese - Egg Fried Rice

60g CARBS	335 CALS

Weight: 180g (half tray)

120g CARBS	670 CALS

Weight: 360g (full tray)

Chinese - Spring Roll

5g CARBS	52 CALS

Weight: 24g

15g CARBS	152 CALS

Weight: 70g

Chinese - Spare Ribs

20g CARBS	405 CALS

Weight: 150g (half tray)

40g CARBS	824 CALS

Weight: 305g (full tray)

Chip Shop - Fish

16g CARBS | **333** CALS

Weight: 135g

Chip Shop - Chips

40g CARBS | **311** CALS

Weight: 130g

39g CARBS | **815** CALS

Weight: 330g

80g CARBS | **626** CALS

Weight: 262g

Battered Sausage

30g CARBS | **410** CALS

Weight: 137g

120g CARBS | **944** CALS

Weight: 395g

Indian - Onion Bhaji

| 15g CARBS | 205 CALS | 15g CARBS | 205 CALS |

Weight: 66g   Weight: 66g

Indian - Pakora

| 5g CARBS | 52 CALS | 10g CARBS | 106 CALS |

Weight: 22g   Weight: 45g

Indian - Samosa (meat)

| 6g CARBS | 82 CALS | 11g CARBS | 158 CALS |

Weight: 30g   Weight: 58g

Indian - Chicken Tikka Masala

| 5g CARBS | 290 CALS | 10g CARBS | 581 CALS |

Weight: 185g (half tray)   Weight: 370g (full tray)

Indian - King Prawn Bhuna

| 5g CARBS | 133 CALS | 10g CARBS | 266 CALS |

Weight: 175g (half tray)   Weight: 350g (full tray)

Indian - Lamb Rogan Josh

| 10g CARBS | 306 CALS | 20g CARBS | 613 CALS |

Weight: 175g (half tray)   Weight: 350g (full tray)

Indian - Bombay Potatoes

15g CARBS   **164** CALS   **30g** CARBS   **327** CALS

Weight: 150g (half tray)   Weight: 300g (full tray)

Indian - Sag Aloo Gobi

10g CARBS   **164** CALS   **20g** CARBS   **328** CALS

Weight: 130g (half tray)   Weight: 260g (full tray)

Indian - Sweet Mango Chutney

10g CARBS   **39** CALS   **20g** CARBS   **80** CALS

Weight: 16g   Weight: 33g

Doner Kebab (small)
50g CARBS   **580** CALS

Weight: 250g

Doner Kebab (large)
80g CARBS   **1053** CALS

Weight: 415g

Shish Kebab (small)
50g CARBS   **435** CALS

Weight: 250g

Shish Kebab (large)
80g CARBS   **762** CALS

Weight: 415g

Falafel in Pitta (small)
60g CARBS   **372** CALS

Weight: 200g

Falafel in Pitta (large)
100g CARBS   **647** CALS

Weight: 350g

Pizza (meat, deep pan)

21g CARBS 176 CALS

	CARBS	CALS
2x	42g	352
3x	63g	528
4x	84g	704
Weight: 70g		

41g CARBS 353 CALS

	CARBS	CALS
2x	82g	706
3x	123g	1059
4x	164g	1412
Weight: 140g		

62g CARBS 524 CALS

	CARBS	CALS
2x	124g	1048
3x	186g	1572
4x	248g	2096
Weight: 208g		

82g CARBS 698 CALS

	CARBS	CALS
2x	164g	1396
3x	246g	2094
4x	328g	2792
Weight: 277g		

Pizza (vegetable, thin crust)

13g CARBS · 126 CALS

	CARBS	CALS
2x	26g	252
3x	39g	378
4x	52g	504
Weight: 50g		

26g CARBS · 252 CALS

	CARBS	CALS
2x	52g	504
3x	78g	756
4x	104g	1008
Weight: 100g		

39g CARBS · 378 CALS

	CARBS	CALS
2x	78	756
3x	117g	1134
4x	156g	1512
Weight: 150g		

52g CARBS · 504 CALS

	CARBS	CALS
2x	104g	1008
3x	156g	1512
4x	208g	2016
Weight: 200g		

Pizza (pepperoni, stuffed crust)

20g CARBS   170 CALS

	CARBS	CALS
2x	40g	340
3x	60g	510
4x	80g	680
Weight: 65g		

40g CARBS   339 CALS

	CARBS	CALS
2x	80g	678
3x	120g	1017
4x	160g	1356
Weight: 130g		

60g CARBS   517 CALS

	CARBS	CALS
2x	120g	1034
3x	180g	1551
4x	240g	2068
Weight: 198g		

80g CARBS   684 CALS

	CARBS	CALS
2x	160g	1368
3x	240g	2052
4x	320g	2736
Weight: 262g		

Thai - Green Curry

| 10g CARBS | 197 CALS | 20g CARBS | 394 CALS |

Weight: 195g (half tray)   Weight: 390g (full tray)

Thai - Phad Thai

| 49g CARBS | 325 CALS | 97g CARBS | 649 CALS |

Weight: 200g (half tray)   Weight: 400g (full tray)

Thai - Pineapple, Chicken & Prawn Rice

| 75g CARBS | 550 CALS | 150g CARBS | 1100 CALS |

Weight: 250g (half tray)   Weight: 500g (full tray)

Baked Beans in Tomato Sauce

10g CARBS   **55 CALS**

Weight: 65g

20g CARBS   **109 CALS**

Weight: 130g

30g CARBS   **164 CALS**

Weight: 195g (half tin)

40g CARBS   **218 CALS**

Weight: 260g

50g CARBS   **273 CALS**

Weight: 325g

60g CARBS   **328 CALS**

Weight: 390g (full tin)

Chick Peas

5g CARBS   **35** CALS

Weight: 30g

Lentils

10g CARBS   **63** CALS

Weight: 60g

10g CARBS   **69** CALS

Weight: 60g

20g CARBS   **126** CALS

Weight: 120g

20g CARBS   **144** CALS

Weight: 125g

30g CARBS   **189** CALS

Weight: 180g

Kidney Beans

| 5g CARBS | 30 CALS |

Weight: 30g

| 10g CARBS | 55 CALS |

Weight: 55g

| 20g CARBS | 115 CALS |

Weight: 115g

Mung Beans

| 5g CARBS | 27 CALS |

Weight: 30g

| 10g CARBS | 59 CALS |

Weight: 65g

| 15g CARBS | 86 CALS |

Weight: 95g

Peas

5g CARBS | **35 CALS**

Weight: 50g

10g CARBS | **69 CALS**

Weight: 100g

15g CARBS | **104 CALS**

Weight: 150g

Mushy Peas

10g CARBS | **61 CALS**

Weight: 75g

20g CARBS | **117 CALS**

Weight: 145g

40g CARBS | **243 CALS**

Weight: 300g

Parsnips

10g CARBS	82 CALS

Weight: 60g

20g CARBS	156 CALS

Weight: 115g

30g CARBS	238 CALS

Weight: 175g

Butternut Squash

10g CARBS	42 CALS

Weight: 130g

20g CARBS	85 CALS

Weight: 265g

30g CARBS	128 CALS

Weight: 400g

Sweetcorn

10g CARBS	46 CALS

Weight: 38g

Corn on the Cob

5g CARBS	29 CALS

Weight: 44g

20g CARBS	92 CALS

Weight: 75g

10g CARBS	56 CALS

Weight: 85g

40g CARBS	183 CALS

Weight: 150g

20g CARBS	112 CALS

Weight: 170g

Plantain (fried)

20g CARBS **112 CALS**

Weight: 42g

40g CARBS **224 CALS**

Weight: 84g

60g CARBS **336 CALS**

Weight: 126g

Yam (boiled)

20g CARBS **80 CALS**

Weight: 60g

40g CARBS **160 CALS**

Weight: 120g

60g CARBS **242 CALS**

Weight: 182g

Index

Manage your Home Build &Renovation Project

How to create your dream home on time, in budget and without stress

David Cambridge

lıp

First published in 2013 by:

Live It Publishing
27 Old Gloucester Road
London, United Kingdom.
WC1N 3AX
www.liveitpublishing.com

978-1-906954-74-1 (pbk)

"For Sue, the foundation of my life and George & Harry,
the windows to my world"

CONTENTS

INTRODUCTION

HOW THIS BOOK CAME ABOUT

Having been in the construction industry for just about 30 years I have seen a lot of what goes on both good and bad through the design, management and the practices of the builder on site. I spent most of these years dealing with a wide range of work including offices, hotels, hospitals and even a power station. I moved into the domestic housing side when I chose to become more involved in local work, ending those days of the city commute and getting the better work life balance everybody talks about.

When I started my residential business I had these grand illusions of dealing with smart home extensions and refurbishments – taking the customers ideas from the very starting point of a project and seeing it through until reaching that dream completion.

Of course, I do get to do those but at that time I had given little consideration to dealing with projects that were in trouble! However, as the business developed I found that I was being asked more and more to step into projects by distressed home owners where things were not going well; be it the builder had disappeared from site, the works were of a poor standard or the project costs appeared to be rising and rising out of control.

We have all seen those distressing television programmes where rogue, cowboy builders have ripped off home owners, delivered poor works then disappeared into the sunset with the customers money never to be seen again. I had always thought that these jobs were the real exceptions in the industry and that generally people were not that stupid. Well I have to admit, I was totally wrong! I continue to come across examples almost on a daily basis where builders are taking people's money whilst delivering unbelievably poor work.

I hate seeing this happen, it makes me sad for the people it has happened to and angry that unscrupulous people can be so callous about doing it. Worst still, it frustrates me that I am unable to help everyone.

That is why I have written this book. I hope that it will help anyone planning to have works done on their home to **get it done the right way** and allow it to be an enjoyable experience. I have presented it in a simple structured manner with easy to understand wording. The book is specifically written for those with little or no construction experience, but even those who have plenty of experience could still do with some help along the way.

Implementing the information in this book will allow you to have a safe and stress free project, I have no doubt that it will also save you money!

Good luck with your project. Enjoy the experience!

HOW TO USE THIS BOOK

I have written this book to allow you to easily refer to it as you move along the project process. Each chapter provides specific guidance on the topic allowing you to dip in and out of it as you need. You will find some parts straightforward, other aspects you may not be so aware of. You can therefore tailor your needs depending on the level of your existing knowledge and experience.

What I would say to start with is to **read through the book from start to finish once before you do anything else.** Don't make the common mistake of skipping sections that you already think you know. It will help you to refresh yourself and you may well find that you pick up extra tips and knowledge along the way.

Don't forget that **one of the biggest reasons why projects fail is that people try to skip activities.** They think they already know what they are doing or that doing the level necessary is overkill for their project or simply that the problems that may arise just won't happen to them! People without the construction experience just do not appreciate the benefits and skills the services professionals perform; especially the management and design team and try to avoid appointing them to save money. This invariably results in a much greater cost to the project; costs that come in late to the project and often when the budget and the homeowner cannot support it!

Many of the projects where I am called in to help are for professional people, accountants, solicitors and the like who think they are above such drama's. Sadly, they do not appreciate the reasons, benefits and worst of all the consequences of each aspect of the project until it is too late! Even if you think you know what you are doing taking a couple of minutes to read through the section, even if just to satisfy yourself, could save you a massive amount of stress and money down the line.

Once you have completed the read through you will have a much better appreciation of what is ahead and the areas that will need most of your attention. Thereafter, as the project progresses you can refer to the individual sections within book to allow you to plan ahead in the short term and also as a reference document.

Don't be scared to write notes over the book as you make decisions and take action, feel free to **tick the sections off as you encounter them in your project and address them.** It will keep you disciplined and motivated. As you progress through the book and your project you will find a greater sense of satisfaction and achievement.

PREPARING
YOURSELF

MAKE YOURSELF A COMITTMENT TO DO IT RIGHT

You have already made a positive start by taking the time to get hold of this book.

There is always the excitement together with a bit of trepidation about undertaking project works to your home but above all **you need to make sure that you protect your property, manage your costs and ensure things are done in a safe and compliant manner.**

I have already outlined in the previous section that skipping aspects of the project is a massive risk therefore if you are truly serious about protecting what is important to you; **you have to be prepared to do things right throughout the course of the project.**

It is no good starting out full of good intentions only to become lazy along the way, be professional. If this was your job you would be governed by business processes and systems, there are correct ways of doing things and you must be accountable. You cannot go and just spend your employers' money without the necessary authority and approval so treat your project in exactly the same way.

Why not even make this commitment to yourself now?

I ....

commit myself to undertake this project in a professional,
disciplined manner from Start to Finish.

Signed ....

Date ....

GIVE YOURSELF ENOUGH TIME

Making sure you have set yourself sufficient time to get the project done properly is essential.

I see it time and time again, people think about having a project done for a long, long time. They read endless magazines, they go to home improvement and property shows, they scribble up their own design layout ideas, they even buy items of equipment and furniture almost on a whim in advance of the project then after ages of dreaming and procrastinating about committing to it they suddenly make the decision to go ahead. Then they want it on site almost immediately, probably before they change their mind, often going straight to a builder and missing out the most important detailed design stage.

Don't fall into this trap. Remember you have just made a commitment to yourself to do this project properly so don't fall at the first hurdle.

Sit down and map out a proper project timescale giving you enough time to get the design done. Make sure that you **allow enough time to obtain the necessary planning and regulation**

approvals, adequate time to select and get a builder on board and the necessary time to do the works to the right standard.

Remember to think about the timing of when the works will be done. What will the weather conditions be like when you need to take the roof off or knock through a side wall? What about school holidays or other important family events? Give yourself a clear picture of when the works will be done and how this can fit into an achievable programme.

Having thought about this the worst thing that you can do is try to rush the up-front design stage to force the project... unless, of course, you have no choice but to do so. Remember undertaking these works will have long lasting results so it is always better to allow a realistic time frame, get it done right and have years of enjoyment, rather than rushing it, making compromises and having years of problems and frustration not to mention the inevitable self-disappointment and anger for not having taken your time.

Equally do not fall into the alternative trap of just never getting it done! Make sure that you **set clear deliverable milestones for completing each stage so that you maintain progress.** When you hit these targets you will find yourself feeling a great level of satisfaction and success.

Finally, remember that **you also have a legal obligation to provide sufficient time to allow the works to be done in a safe manner.** You cannot force a builder to undertake works in a manner that offers an unacceptable risk, even if it should get to a stage when they are behind programme and have to catch up (which hopefully should not happen if you are doing things right!).

ACCEPT YOUR CAPABILITIES

Being clear and honest about what you are capable of doing and accepting where you need help is fundamental.

It always amazes me how often I have been brought in to help get a project back on track by people who have been trying to do aspects of management and construction themselves when they simply do not have the necessary skills, knowledge and experience.

Think about it:

Do you have the construction experience and technical skills to understand the details allowing you to make the right decisions and also know when things that are being presented to you are right or wrong? Are you immediately putting yourself at a disadvantage and at risk?

Do you have the contract management skills necessary to implement contractual appointments and prepare building contracts that will adequately protect you, your property and your money?

Do you have the necessary communication skills and confidence to be able to deal with professionals and the builders? What if things are not going well or the builder starts demanding more money? Are you able to manage the situation?

Do you have the necessary time available to put into the project to make it happen? People always under-estimate the time involved to get the project delivered competently.

Are you disciplined enough to effectively manage changes and variations or are you impatient and want things done now?

Are you emotionally controlled because works to the home can feel personal and you need to be able to control your emotions in order to make effective decisions and deal appropriately with the builder.

There are a number of reasons why people end up doing aspects of the project that they should not be, the most common of these are:

They do not know where to go for the best advice – well after reading this book that should no longer be an excuse!

They want to save money – trying to do things out of your skill set will be more costly as well as less time efficient. Make sure you have adequate budget up front to allow the necessary skills to be bought in. If you don't have sufficient budget then you probably should not be doing the works to start with as, inevitably, you will find yourself in financial problems later if you have not sufficient funds to do it right from the start.

They think they can do it all themselves – Well now is the time to be honest with yourself before it's too late!

You wouldn't try and service your car (not nowadays anyway) would you? You take it to a garage. You wouldn't give yourself a dental filling; you would go to the dentist so why on earth would you attempt to run a project which is of a much greater financial impact than the cost of your car or the cost of a filling if you do not have the necessary skills and experience?

Be clear and honest with yourself, what parts of the project are you happy doing yourself and where do you need help?

PLANNING YOUR PROJECT

SETTING YOUR PROJECT OBJECTIVES

If you want your project to deliver what you ultimately need you need to have a clear understanding or **what you want** and **why you want it**. You should also consider what the short and long term benefits are and how ultimately you will measure **the success of your project**. You may also want to set out the aspects of the project that you specifically do not want to happen.

Remember the reasons people have works done to their home are very personal so you need to make sure your objectives are right for you.

When I sit down with my clients this is always an area that gives them the most trouble, yet if you are not clear of this then how on earth are you ever going to reach your desired outcome? And more so, how can you expect other people helping you deliver your project to give you what you want?

So think about it and write it down, maybe along the following lines:

WHAT DO YOU WANT?

- Scope – A new master bedroom with an en suite bathroom in the loft space.
- Lifestyle – We want our own luxurious bathroom with a big bath / shower.
- Timing – The works to be completed by our youngest son's 9th Birthday in October.
- Style – A high quality of finish with a modern style.
- Features – Lots of natural sunlight.
- Important considerations – To maximise the floor to ceiling height so it does not feel oppressive.
- Feel – The works to be completed so they are seen as a natural part of the house, not an add-on therefore a proper staircase and similar finishes.
- Price – A total budget for the works including all fees, statutory approvals, fittings and additional costs such as temporary accommodation.

WHY DO YOU WANT IT?

- To create an additional bedroom to the house so our two children do not have to share a room as they grow up.
- Because we like the area and do not want to move.

- We do not want to have an extension because we want to still keep a large garden.
- To show off to the neighbours.

WHAT ARE THE SHORT TERM BENEFITS?

- More space for the family.
- Both children can have their own space.
- We as parents get a smart new bedroom.
- The children don't have to change schools.

WHAT ARE THE LONG TERM BENEFITS?

- To increase the value of our home, the works are an investment.
- The works will allow the home to be more appealing to future potential buyers if we choose to sell.

What YOU DO NOT want

- A restricted staircase.
- The works undertaken during the cold winter months Nov – March.
- To exceed the budget.

UNDERSTAND YOUR PRIORITIES & DECISION MAKING

Being able to **make consistent, conscious decisions** is essential if you are going to be able to develop your project designs in a timely and effective manner.

Too often people are uncomfortable about making choices and when they do they still feel uncomfortable about them, even when they are making the correct ones! This is to be fully understood, after all these decisions will literally be set in stone and therefore in something that they will have to live with for a long time so making sure that the right choices is an important part of the process.

Being able to do this in a clear conscious manner **will add confidence and significantly reduce the stress levels** through the process.

To help support this aspect it is worth appreciating that on any project there are three overriding aspects:

- Time
- Cost, and
- Quality.

You may choose to have a high quality of finish to your project whilst looking to keep costs down however this will have a consequence on the project programme as you may have to find more time to undertake more of the works yourself or allow the builder to fit in aspects of your project during his quiet periods so you can get them at a reduced rate.

Alternatively, time may be essential to you as is the high quality of the work; you will therefore have to pay a premium for urgent shipping of materials, out of hours working by tradesmen etc.

I would therefore suggest that you take time to set out your views on these aspects in line with your identified project objectives:

Time: when and how quickly do you want the project undertaken? Are there critical timescales that have to be met? To what extent are you prepared to let the project period extend?

Cost: What is your project budget and how does this impact on the scope of works that you want? Are you prepared to be flexible on costs or do you have an absolute budget? You will also need to consider the cash flow for the project, when will you have the money available to fund the works?

Quality: What level of quality of fixtures and fittings do you expect? Are you looking for high tech state of the art items or are you happy with standard stock items?

Now, considering the above **what aspects of the project are a must** and you are not prepared to compromise. Equally **what aspects are you prepared to be flexible** on?

There is no reason why you cannot apply this thinking to the project as an overall activity but equally break the project down to a number of sub elements, i.e. you might want a tight project timescale overall but you will not compromise on having the top of the range audio entertainment system installed or that bespoke kitchen? If this is the case you will need to accept that previously identified aspects of the project may need re-thinking and re-prioritising to achieve those things you are not prepared to compromise.

The most important point, however, is that you have clear requirements at the outset and you make your decisions consciously, consistently in alignment with your requirements and therefore with good reason.

MAINTAINING A PROJECT PLAN

Keeping a project plan will allow you to maintain control and keep an organised record of all aspects of your project. While in essence it is a filing record of your project it should be extended to make sure that it incorporates your personal requirements and decisions.

The Project Plan can really be based upon the structure of this book; I have deliberately written it this way to help you.

So, let's be clear exactly what the benefits of maintaining a Project Plan are:

Contractual Administration. It should be a complete filing system for all documentation relating to the project. This will include:

- Project directory & contact list
- Correspondence. Don't just limit this to letters, make sure all emails, faxes and even records of verbal discussions (which I strongly recommend are always confirmed back in writing afterwards) are included
- Contract documents & appointments

- Notices of Contractual variations and changes
- Statutory approvals, licences and notices
- Design Information including drawings, specifications, manufacturers literation and guides
- Insurance records

Financial Control. It will allow you to keep a close track of the project costs making sure that you keep to budget and control cash flow and should include the following:

- The project budget and project cash flow
- Records of all quotations and tender bids
- Financial records of Contractual variations and changes, and
- Applications for payment, invoices and payment receipts

Programme Management. To make sure that you understand the milestones of your project are met and keep you aware of the following:

- Overall project plan
- Milestones – key dates and outcomes
- Critical equipment and delivery lead in periods, and
- Aspects of critical disruptive works
- Project Progress Reports

Now the above are the standard aspects of project management control that are necessary for a successful project but I would also strongly recommend you thinking about the following additional benefits of good project planning and management:

Confidence and Control. Having detailed records to hand in a well-managed structural manner will allow you to have the upper hand when it comes to discussions with project members such as the builder if they start looking for additional payments.

Focus. You will have clear direction for the project, which make it easier for you to stay on track in terms of time and money.

Saving time. It will allow you to make decisions in a more timely manner and prevent delays when you are trying to find information and historic records.

Managing risks and responding to incidents effectively. Having information easily to hand will allow you to address issues, either physical problems on site or managing commercial matters.

DOING YOUR RESEARCH

The better you are able to brief people helping you with your project the quicker you will be able to reach the right outcome.

Whilst the professional team will be able to add the technical and physical construction expertise, ultimately as the home owner you are the one that is going to live with the end product. You therefore have a massive role in making sure that all people involved in the project have a clear understanding of what you want and that that is what they are delivering for you!

You have started out on the right track by getting this book, now is the time to list out all of the specific design aspects of the project that you want incorporated within your scheme.

It is equally worth looking at the outline costs so you have a feel what is likely to be realistic and identify possible options that could be considered if you find you need to make budgetary savings, or even better you find you have more funds available for an upgrade.

Here are a number of aspects I suggest you focus your research on:

National Planning. Review the government on-line planning portal. This will provide you with a good indication what aspects of a project require Planning approval and what can be considered a permitted development. The portal is very interactive and easy to use.

Local Planning. Whilst the planning portal is a good indication you will still need to take account of your local area, especially if you are in designated green belt land or a conservation area. Try to get an appreciation of what other developments have taken place locally, in your street and your neighbourhood. This will provide you with a good indicator of what the local council are likely to accept from a planning perspective.

Local Authority Consultation. Local planning officers used to be happy to have general discussions about ideas you may have for construction. Nowadays they are still happy to have a consultation meeting with you however you now have to pay for this service. If you are planning to undertake a development where you have not seen any local precedent (i.e. examples of other people who have done the same type of development near you), then you may be considering something that is pushing the boundaries of the planning requirements. If this is the case, or if you are considering developing something unusual then it is always worth paying for this service before expending a lot of money on professional design services.

Look at Other Similar Projects. If there are other people in your street that have had a similar type of work undertaken that you are considering I would make sure that you take the time to speak to them and ideally look in detail at the works they have done. This can be incredibly useful as it will give you a real appreciation of what can be done: what you like and will work for you and of course what you don't like and won't work for you. It will give you a much better appreciation of how it all works as opposed to trying to make sense of it all by looking at plans on a drawing. You will get a much better understanding of aspects such as: scale, use of space, how natural and artificial light will impact on the area and so forth.

In my experience people that have had a great project undertaken love talking about them and showing them off. They will also be able to talk to you about the real areas of difficulty, especially during the construction period and what to prepare for.

Measure Things Up. Take time to measure up items of furniture and equipment that you want included within your project space so that you understand the area that things will take up including the amount of space that will be required around them. Remember to consider how things will be mounted and any supporting services that will be required such as power sockets, aerial connections. You also need to consider the impact of lighting, both natural and artificial. Typical items to consider include beds (single, doubles and king size), the number of kitchen cupboards and appliances, large televisions and other entertainment equipment. Also think about the future, televisions seem to get larger and larger all the time so make sure your project is future proofed!

Service Layouts. Make sure you provide for all the necessary power points, TV aerial locations, telephone and data points as well as all the gas, electric, water and drainage. You also need to consider how your project can be served from the existing services provisions.

Drainage holds by far the most limiting restrictions due to the demands of natural drainage levels. Think about where your existing drainage runs are and how easy, or not, it will be to connect new kitchens and bathrooms to them. This may have a significant impact on your layouts, especially if it means you have to locate these particular rooms on a specific side of the house so that drainage connections can be made. In the worst cases you may well be forced to install a further drain connection to the local company sewer, which can be a costly activity, or provide pumping which again will be a costly investment and will also require on-going maintenance thereafter. Some alternative means of drainage disposal may need to be considered such as the use of a septic tank.

Styles, Finishes and Fittings. Get an understanding of the type and style of finishes that you want incorporated within this project. Remember that they need to compliment the remainder of the house and the area, particularly in respect of external aspects if planning approval is required.

An effective way of managing your choice of finishes and portraying this to your project team is to create either a scrapbook holding clippings of the finishes you want taken from magazines and brochures or better still a finishes board with samples.

Make sure you include elements such as door and window styles; door and window sundries such as handles and locks; skirting's and architraves; light fittings, switches and power sockets; kitchen units, handles and worktops; sanitary fittings, taps and decorative finishes including floor coverings, paintwork and furnishings.

Technology Solutions. Technology plays a greater and greater part of our home living style. You therefore need to have a clear view of equipment and systems that you want incorporated within your project from the early stages. Items such as home cinemas and integrated control systems are becoming more and more affordable but incorporating them within your project requires careful planning. It is much easier to install cable routes and power suppliers during the main build rather than trying to install them retrospectively.

PROJECT
DESIGN
OPTIONS

THE DESIGN STAGES

There are 5 key stages to the design development of your project.

- Site Survey and Investigation
- Feasibility & Sketch Design
- Planning
- Detailed Design
- Supplementary Design Packages

Too often people embarking on a project are not aware of these distinct stages which leads to the following **two common project mistakes** which I see time and time again:

Firstly, **they do not spend enough time on the feasibility** and want to head straight to Planning Stage. This means that they do not fully consider the options available to them and ultimately end up making compromises along the way.

The second is **not spending enough time on the detailed design** stage before tendering with the builders and construction. They have the set of planning drawings; develop these enough for submission for Building Regulation Notice but still leave a lot of design and specification to take place as the works are being constructed. The results of this can have serious consequences on the success of the project. The builder recognises the lack of detail and therefore prices elements of "risk" within his costs, this means ultimately the client is paying over and above the actual cost for nothing! Design development then takes place as the works progress when you suddenly realise aspects do not work, power sockets are in the wrong place, drainage connections don't match toilet layouts. All sorts of problems can arise which lead to variations, stripping out and replacing work already undertaken, ultimately resulting in increased costs, delays to programme and lots of frustration and anger!

This is at the heart of why projects go wrong!

SITE SURVEY AND INVESTIGATION

When embarking on a project you need to have a clear understanding of where you are starting from, what constraints the existing site has, what you have to work with and what conditions you need to overcome.

The extent of any site survey and investigation will be dependent upon the nature of the project but will broadly need to cover the following:

The size and topography of the site. Determine the boundaries, ground levels, falls, ground type, access routes, and rights of way. You might want to investigate other potential aspects that you consider will have a restriction on the extent of works you can undertake. For example, if your property is located in a conservation area or is a listed building.

Existing structures, foundations and type of construction. This is especially if you are planning to use part of the existing structure as a load bearing element for your project area.

The existing services infrastructure, both in respect of the **utility provision** to the site, gas, water, electricity and drainage and also the **internal systems and distribution**, heating, water services, power lighting, telephones and cable / satellite TV. Remember it is not just important to know where they are, you need to be aware of their capacities and if they are able to provide the additional loads required of them from your project works.

Drainage is always one of the most important considerations in this respect. Due to the need to provide drainage, preferably by means of gravity, the depth of the main drain runs below ground and the ability to connect them can be one of the most limiting aspects in determining your design plans. They may seriously impact where you locate your bathrooms and kitchens and especially where they are situated on the ground floor. You can always provide pumping but this will mean a significant additional cost, take up more space where you need to locate the pumping equipment, can often be noisy and will also mean on-going maintenance and a greater risk of breakdown of one of the most important aspects of your home.

FEASIBILITY AND SKETCH DESIGN

Before embarking on significant design costs it is worth undertaking a sketch design process. You can quickly look at the different options and ideas that you have for your project and get a feel for what can be achieved. I would always recommend that you undertake this in two stages.

Stage 1 – Freehand Layout Concepts

The first stage is to do some very simple freehand sketches yourself, look at the plan layouts, ideally to a scale of about 1:50 and draw up ideas of how the rooms would work together, think about the following factors as a check list:

- How the flow of the house works from room to room. The relationship between the kitchen and dining room – avoiding noisy areas such as a utility rooms being close to your relaxed living area for example

- Access routes in and out of the house or to a garage – do you have to take your rubbish bags through the house to the bins?

- How sunlight will impact on the house throughout the day. Try and maximise the use of natural light

- The size and layouts of each room. How big will they need to be, where will the furniture fit, where will you position focal points such as where to site a television?

- How you will use the room. What are your views and what views will outsiders have of your home – do you want to be sitting in a dining area at the front of your house where people passing can watch you eat?

- How much storage you need and will this consist of specific constructed rooms or cupboards or will you use furniture within the space?

- The location of services such as radiators (ideally below windows), hot and cold water, drainage, power sockets, lighting etc.

- The security of the house. Maybe you have an office. If so, don't put your valuable equipment at the front which will attract burglars.

Stage 2 – Developing Your Ideas into Working Sketch Plans

Unless you have both a good construction background and an artistic flair this would be the initial stage when I would recommend that you employ the services of an architect to assist you with your project.

Having worked through your own freehand sketch designs you will have learnt a lot about what you want and the specific factors that are important to you and this will allow you to share these thoughts and requirements through a good briefing. Always remember to include both what you want, and just as importantly what you want to avoid!

The architect can then take these sketch plans and generate a more detailed sketch design. I would always look for them to generate sketch layout plans, elevations and ideally some visual sketches or computer generated 3D pictures of what the spaces will look like. These can help you get a much better appreciation of what the project will look like than a cold black and white building plan layout. **Always remember that whatever you ultimately have designed you will have to live with for years to come so making sure that the design is right is an absolute must!** It's always a lot easier to adjust and amend things on paper than it is during or after construction.

Bringing in an architect will also allow this stage to consider the practicability of construction. They will be able to consider the structure, especially the location of load bearing walls that will have an impact on what you can and cannot do with your home. Of course everything is ultimately possible but adapting the structural loading of the building will always have greater financial consequences. It will also allow you to consider opportunities for cost control and indicative thoughts of what will be achievable within your potential budget.

This will also be the initial point where you are able to consider an application for Outline Planning Approval if your project requires it. This is dealt with a little later in this book.

PLANNING

Having developed your scheme in sketch form the next stage of the design process will be to complete the design package for obtaining Planning Approval (if required). There is much more detail on this and what is required provided in its own section a little later in this book so I will not go deeply into it at this point other than to say that this is the initial main step of the design process where you will formalise your site layout, base project plans and external elevations of the works.

DETAILED DESIGN

As I mentioned at the start of the section this is an area where people consistently fail to invest enough time on their project which later translates into the stories you hear all the time of project costs rising and rising out of control during the construction and the project end date getting later and later. I scream at my client's time and time again **SPEND AS MUCH TIME AS YOU POSSIBLY CAN ON THIS PART OF THE PROJECT AND DETAIL AND SPECIFY AS MUCH AS POSSIBLE NOW IF YOU WANT YOUR PROJECT TO RUN WELL**. You can see I get a bit heated about this but it is so essential!

The detailed design stage has two main purposes:

To ensure the works are sufficiently designed so that they work and are compliant with the Building Regulations.

- To make sure that there is sufficient detail that the builder is in no doubt about what has to be constructed.

The first is a statutory obligation and is dealt with in its own section later in this book so I will not go into that more at this point.

The second is absolutely 100% critical to the success of your project. The more detail that your project design package of drawings and specifications has the clearer that your builder will be on what needs to be constructed. This will mean:

- That he will be able to properly price the cost of the works

- He will not price in unnecessary costs for Risk to deal with unknown or undetermined aspects (this is typically a pot of money that he will allow in his price that is actually not going toward the actual construction therefore you are really paying money for potentially nothing!)

- He will be able to plan a clear method and programme of work which will help organise tradesmen and deliveries when required, pre-order the right amount of materials, fixtures and fittings & properly plan times of disruptive works

- There will be a lot less "designing on the job" which will avoid lots of changes, re-working; stripping out already completed works which would all cause increase in costs and delays to programme

- You will also find that the actual relationship of the project team, including yourself and the builder, will be much better as nobody is being given the run around and people become less reluctant during the construction phase to provide information or do work to tight deadlines

Use this tick-list to make sure that your detailed design encapsulates all of the necessary information

BASE INFORMATION

- Site plan
- Floor plans
- Elevations
- Internal sections

ARCHITECTURAL DESIGN DETAILS

- Specific design details required such as floor make, damp protection and courses, building insulation
- Wall construction details
- Special architectural features
- Decorative finishes to ceilings, walls, floors, skirting's, dado rails, architraves
- Specifications of doors, windows and roof lights including the ironmongery and accessories
- Tiling and other finishes
- Sanitary Fittings
- Kitchen cupboards, fittings and appliances

STRUCTURAL DESIGN DETAILS

- Structural design layouts
- Structural calculations including beam and steelwork schedules
- Specific structural details such as roof structures, wall details and foundations

BUILDING SERVICES DESIGN DETAILS

- Drainage
  - Location of foul and surface water drain runs, manholes and gullies
- Sanitary Disposal
  - Soil and waste pipes and vent points
- Rainwater Disposal
  - Gutters and downpipes
- Domestic Water Services
  - Incoming water main
  - Water metering points
  - Cold water storage
  - Hot water storage
  - Pipework distribution routes including isolation stopcocks and service valves and drain down points.
  - Terminal fittings (taps, showers, hose points etc.)
- Gas
  - Incoming main route
  - Metering
  - Pipework distribution routes and points of isolation
  - Terminal equipment

Heating
- Feed and expansion tanks
- Boilers, including flues
- Pipework distribution routes, isolation and drain down points
- Terminal radiators, towel rails
- Central controllers
- Local thermostats and control points

Power
- Main incoming supply
- Metering
- Distribution fuse boards
- Cable routes
- Terminal power sockets and switches
- Outside power points
- Safety protection devices

Lighting
- Cable routes
- General room lighting points
- Feature lighting
- Security lighting
- Switching points

Earth bonding and earth protection

Telephone, Broadband, Satellite & Cable systems
- Dishes and main incoming data points
- Central controllers, boosters and hubs
- Cable routes
- Terminal fittings

Home Entertainment Systems

🗼 Security Systems
- Alarms
- CCTV

SUPPLEMENTARY DESIGN PACKAGES

In addition to the main overall project detailed design there may be the need to incorporate specialist design packages for certain aspects of the works. These could include:

🗼 Bathrooms

🗼 Kitchens

🗼 Home entertainment systems

🗼 Security systems

I would always recommend that these are done at the same time and incorporated as part of the detailed design process and not done at a later stage in the project. You must not forget that although they may not be installed until near the end of the construction process they may still require significant infrastructure and service work to be installed during the main construction phase to take account of them, especially where drainage, water, power and other cabled services are required.

WHO DOES THE DESIGN?

There are two methods of having the design undertaken which also feed into the type of building contract that you have in place. These are known commonly as:

Traditional

or

Design and Build

The two methods are quite different, it is therefore important that you have a clear appreciation of the two routes from an early stage in your project and are able to dictate how you propose to take your project forward.

THE TRADITIONAL ROUTE

This is where a design team, usually consisting of an architect, structural engineer and building services consultant are employed, preferably through a project manager and develop the full design right through the detailed design process. This provides a clear design solution that the builder will construct. The builder has to build exactly to the requirements and specification of the design and any issues relating to its ability to be constructed or the selection of materials will remain with the design team.

This means that the responsibility for the design remains with the client (which is passed down to the design team) and there is a fixed price for a defined scope of works.

Therefore the client retains the financial risk but maintains control of the project and has the benefit of being **able to dictate the quality and choice of materials** and the **ability to instruct changes as the project progresses.**

The success of the project is therefore down to the quality of the design team to develop a successful and detailed design.

DESIGN AND BUILD

This route is where you specify the project requirements to **the builder who is then responsible for developing the design and delivering your requirements for an agreed price.**

The benefits of this method are that you have transferred all the risks of construction and cost onto the builder. However, although this seems an ideal scenario there are a number of things that need careful consideration before you go down this route:

You have to be very careful how detailed and how explicit you are setting out your project requirements. Once you have established these requirements, obtained the price from the builder and signed the contract **you have lost your ability to control and change the works.** It is entirely down to him how the design is progressed, what choice of materials, fittings and equipment are supplied if you have not already specifically set them.

This could mean that your expectations are not fully met at the end, i.e. you expect to have nice polished stainless steel power sockets and switches but you only actually specified the locations and number of switches and in the end the builder only provides plastic ones.

That is only a very simple example to demonstrate the point but this can be taken to extreme circumstances depending on the vagueness of your output requirements, right up to the shape of the extension, location and type of building materials and even the method of construction.

Once you have signed the Contract the builder does not necessarily have to accept change requests so if during the construction process you find that you want something changed because maybe it is not what you want, for example you think it might work better if a window was moved a little to the right, you have no ability or legal power to make the builder make that change.

WHICH ROUTE DO YOU CHOOSE?

There are obviously places for both methods of design and procurement and it is much about how much you are prepared to transfer the risk and accept a fixed cost against the lack of control.

In my experience the design and build process works very well when you are undertaking project work in a commercial environment either for a business or where you are building a property for someone else to live in.

If you are undertaking a project on your own home and it is where you are going to live for a long time after the project has finished than I would always recommend that you retain the ability to make changes during the work. You might just find that during the construction your requirements change, or something although on paper looks fine but as it is built just does not appear right and you might want to change or add something. The traditional route will give you that ability.

TRADITIONAL PROCUREMENT PROJECT ORGANISATION STRUCTURE

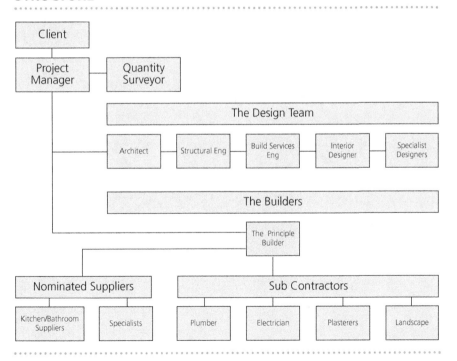

DESIGN & BUILD PROCUREMENT PROJECT ORGANISATION STRUCTURE

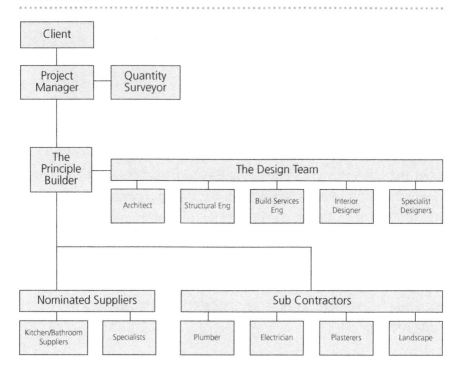

HEALTH & SAFETY COMPLIANCE

Residential work does not fall under the Construction Design and Management Regulations however as a client you still have legal obligations and hold a duty of care to ensure that the works are undertaken in a safe manner.

Your principle obligation as a client is to ensure that you allow sufficient resource to be applied to a project to ensure that it is undertaken in a safe manner. When I say "resource" this generally relates to allowing sufficient time and funds so works are not delivered in haste without the proper planning and allowing necessary time to deliver.

You therefore have to be realistic about what you want to deliver and cannot put your project team into difficult positions. Being realistic about what can be achieved is essential and may require specialist knowledge.

Remember to think about the hazards of having project work undertaken to your home at present. This needs special consideration when you have vulnerable people present such as young children or the elderly; you also need to think about your pets. Make sure that any areas of risk are well managed and ensure that the necessary control measures are put in place with the builder to prevent harm not only to you or your family but also to the builders and other tradespeople.

Below are some of the main hazards that can be found on your building site that you need to be aware of. You would expect the builder to maintain them in a safe condition from a working perspective i.e. preventing trenches collapsing or making sure scaffolding is erected properly and is structurally sound so I will focus on the home owner risks here not the builders.

Excavations and trenches – digging these out can need large plant and equipment and for deeper trenches there is a greater risk of injury from falling into them. Make sure that they are cordoned off if people are likely to go near them especially young unsupervised children or during hours of darkness.

Scaffolding and ladders – make sure that the builder provides the necessary protection or removes the ground floor access when not in use to make sure that they cannot be climbed up.

Plant, equipment and power tools – firstly they should be 110V not 240V and protected by Residual Circuit Breakers. Wherever possible the safety devices guards and shields should be installed and whenever not being used by workmen they should be safely stored away.

Electrical cables – when installations are in the middle of being stripped out or new circuits installed any loose wiring should be coiled up, labelled and placed out of reach.

General debris, rubbish, loose and stored materials – a tidy site is generally a safe site. Make sure that the builder keeps the site in good order. Rubbish is regularly cleaned up during the day and stored in agreed locations in the appropriate containers and skips. Materials and goods must be stored in dry, safe locations and in a manner that prevents them from becoming loose or falling.

APPROVALS
AND
PERMISSIONS

WHAT YOU NEED TO DEAL WITH

There are three main areas to consider when undertaking your project, these are:

- Planning Approval
- Building Regulation Compliance, and
- Party Wall Agreements

Each of these is detailed in the following sections to help you understand what each aspect is and how to deal with them.

Making sure that you have complied with these regulations and controls is essential. There have been many instances where developments have been constructed and subsequently demolished after enforcement notices have been issued because the necessary approvals had not been obtained.

This won't just cost you the money of the construction, there will be a fortune in legal fees not to mention the distress and anguish of seeing your home, which you have toiled over with blood sweat and tears drop to the ground.

PLANNING APPROVAL

WHAT IS IT?

Planning approval is controlled by your local council and is focused on what you build; its compatibility with the surrounding environment and its safety. **Basically what you can build, where**.

It is based on Acts of Parliament, principally the Town & Country Planning Act.

WHEN DO YOU NEED PLANNING APPROVAL

Many works relating to refurbishment, small extensions and loft conversions may not require Planning Approval. For example if you are constructing a loft conversion to the rear of your property that is less than 40m³ then there is a good likelihood that your project will not need Planning approval unless your house is in a conservation area.

The Government provides a very useful website providing advice and guidance on planning requirements. This can be found at www.planningportal.gov.uk. This site provides an excellent interactive graphical representation of a home and the types of typical project works undertaken, if they require permission, and general downloadable guidance reference documents. This site is a **MUST** point of reference to evaluate your planning requirements.

GETTING ADVICE FROM YOUR PLANNING OFFICER

Consultation can be made with your local council Planning Department to discuss your proposed development where they are able to offer you guidance and advice.

This service used to be free but nowadays they will charge you for this service. If you do this through correspondence their basic charge will normally be around £120-£150 for them to write back to you or if you want to have a meeting with them to discuss your plans the cost will be in the region of £350-£400 at the time of writing this book.

Whilst this may initially seem expensive it can be a very useful exercise and ultimately cost effective by saving you money progressing elements of design that have no realistic chance of success. The meetings and advice can also point out key issues that will need to be specifically addressed within the formal application such as access onto the highway that you may not have originally considered or recognised as an important issue within the scope of the project.

BE PERSISTENT WITH YOUR APPLICATION

Planning approvals can at times seem to be hard work and difficult to resolve but perseverance and having the right person on your side with good local knowledge of allowable development requirements is important.

Planning Authorities have a responsibility to the community to maintain the right environment. However, with the on-going political pressures to support the construction industry and help aid the economy there is evidence that planning restrictions are becoming a little more relaxed.

If you receive an initial rejection there is often scope to develop a mutually acceptable solution with some compromise.

TYPES OF PLANNING APPLICATION

There are 6 main types of application, the purpose of each are detailed below:

Outline Planning Permission. This is primarily used where you are considering a project that is offering a fundamental change to what exists; typically a change in use or new development such as constructing a property on an existing field site, a barn conversion and changing the use of a shop or disused pub into a residential dwelling. It can also be used where you are changing the building into a different style or look, especially if it is making a significant architectural statement that is out of keeping with the surrounding area.

The benefits of submitting an outline application is to get good feel as to how the proposed development will be accepted by the Planning authorities without spending significant funds developing a design for a project that has no chance of being accepted.

Approved outline planning permissions are granted for 5 years however detailed Full applications must be agreed within 3 years otherwise the permission expires and the process will have to be started all over again.

Full Planning Application. As the name suggests this is the main process for obtaining approval for your project.

A planning approval will last for a 3 year period before expiry. By the time the 3 years are up works have to have commenced on site for it to remain as a permitted development. The extent of works usually required to be accepted as the project having commenced will be the completion of the foundations.

Amendment Application. During the course of the detailed design development or even during construction changes may arise or at least be considered that will impact on the external layouts, elevations or choice of finishes that formed the original detail of the approved application.

To maintain the approval an amendment to the original application may be sought by submitting a revised package for a nominal fee.

If the Local Authority considers that the changes are substantial they may request a new Full Planning application to be submitted.

Renewal Application. A renewal can be used to obtain an extension to an existing Full Application which is reaching its expiry but the works have been delayed in commencing. This has become more of an issue in recent years as funding has been more difficult to obtain putting planned developments on hold.

Whilst renewals are available they must be fully completed prior to the expiry date of the original approval and you also need to be aware that if since the original approval was granted significant changes to the surrounding area have taken place the renewal may not be granted if the proposed development plans are no longer compatible with the area.

Approval of Reserved Matters. This process would be used to convert items specifically identified within an Outline Planning Approval into a full application. Typical aspects that may fall into this include addressing rights of way, highway access or wildlife and environmental impact assessments.

Relaxations. Sometimes Applications may be approved but come with a number of specific requirements that will need to be addressed or included within the project. These may be lifted if ultimately you can demonstrate that you have good reasons for these to no longer be applicable or relevant but in general such relaxations are normally pretty difficult to obtain and I would not get your hopes up in respect of avoiding doing the works to comply.

HOW TO SUBMIT A PLANNING APPLICATION

The process for submitting an application is relatively easy to undertake.

Each local council will have a "Planning" section on their website which will provide you with all the necessary guidance as to how to submit your application, the template documents you will be required to complete and a table of fees to be applied.

Many Local Authorities now allow you to make your submission on-line so make sure that you get copies of all relevant documents including drawings, specifications and reports in an electronic format, ideally converted to PDF for ease of submission.

Once your application has been submitted a Planning Officer will be designated to your case to deal with all correspondence and issues in relation to your approval process.

Depending on the nature of your project the planning officer will come and inspect the area of the proposed works for them to satisfy themselves that your proposals are appropriate for the area and comply with the requirements of the Planning Act. They may already know your area well and if the works are of a basic nature and similar to many other projects that have already been completed in your road / area then they may not need a specific visit.

The Local Authority will also notify your neighbours and any other local residents that may possibly be affected by your proposed works who will have the opportunity to consider and make comment / objection to your intended project.

Just because they may submit a negative view of your proposal does not mean that it will necessarily be rejected. It is up to the Planning Officer to consider the application and ultimately submit a recommendation to the council chamber for approval or for it to be declined.

Throughout the period of the application process you will be able to monitor progress and correspondence on the Local Authority website.

WHAT NEEDS TO BE INCLUDED IN A PLANNING APPLICATION?

The following are the standard sets of information required for a planning application submission that you will be expected to provide.

The Application Form. This can be downloaded from the planning section of the Local Authority website. It is normally a fairly simple form to complete and provides contact information of the applicant, and your agent if you are using one, and very simple information regarding the proposed works.

The Payment. This can normally be paid through an on-line payment system or by sending a cheque to the council offices.

The Site Location Plan. This will be based on an Ordinance Survey Map at a scale of 1:1250. Note that the existing site boundaries will need to be highlighted in a red line on the application plan.

The Existing Site Plan. This will be presented on a drawing at a scale of 1:500 and again will have to have the site boundaries highlighted in red. This drawing should detail all buildings, structures, trees, landscaping and access routes to the highway. It is also beneficial to survey and identify all the utility services, especially drainage routes on this plan.

The Proposed Site Plan. This will be presented on a drawing at a scale of 1:500. It will show the layout of your proposed building (including the existing to remain and the new construction), trees (highlighting any existing that are to be removed as a result of the project), landscaping, access routes and any revised proposals to the boundaries.

Layouts of Existing Structures. Floor plans of each level of the building(s) at a scale of 1:50.

Elevations of Existing Structures and the Site. This will be required for each elevation of the site (normally front, rear and each side but dependent on the actual shape of the area). These will be presented at a scale of 1:50.

Layouts of the Proposed Structures. Floor plans of each level of the building(s) at a scale of 1:50.

Elevations of the Proposed Structures. As per the existing plans at a scale of 1:50.

The drawings should be sufficiently noted to provide details of materials and finishes as existing and to be used in the new construction.

ADDITIONAL INFORMATION THAT MAY BE REQUIRED.

It is best to consider in advance any information that the planning officer is likely to require to support the decision making process. Typical items of additional information that may be required include:

 A schedule of trees to be felled

 Highways and access impact assessment to evaluate the site entry and access, especially if you are creating or re-constructing routes onto a highway, boundary walls and fences or gates. Consideration will need to be made regarding the impact of vehicles slowing down to enter the site, how they pull on to the highway and especially relating to lines of sight and the ability to see vehicles approaching and for vehicles to see traffic pulling out

- An environmental impact assessment if there are issues relating to specific wildlife and water courses
- Listed buildings and conservation areas will have their own specific requirements that will need to be met

BUILDING REGULATIONS

WHAT ARE THEY?

The Building Regulations are a set of technical documents that set the standards to which construction must be delivered in accordance with, in order to meet an acceptable level in respect of structural soundness, safety, environmental impact and quality.

As opposed to the Planning Approvals which deal with what you can build, and where, the **Building Regulations address how your project is built**.

The Building Regulations come in a set of approved Documents Parts A-P, each addressing a specific element of construction as follows:

A   Structure
B   Fire
C   Waterproofing
D   Cavity Insulation
E   Sound
F   Ventilation

G Hygiene

H Drains & Fuel

J Flues & Chimneys

K Stairs

L Energy Use

M Access

N Glazing

P Electrics

The complete set of Building Regulation documents can be purchased for £60, they are also available for download for free from the governments planning portal.

If you are using the traditional design and procurement approach your project design team will have a responsibility to ensure that their designs are compliant with the Regulations.

I think it is fair to also note that most builders are not particularly well aware of the details of the Building Regulations. That is not to say that they will not construct their works in a compliant manner but based on what they have learned over time in doing the job. They will therefore rely on the level of detail provided in the design pack and specifications provided to them from the design team and also from the guidance of the building control inspectors monitoring their site works.

MAKING A BUILDING REGULATION SUBMISSION

Just as with Planning, Building Regulations compliance is generally controlled by your Local Authority who's Building Control Department has a number of Building Inspectors. Alternatively there are a number of Building Control Agents who are private companies that are licenced to provide this service.

Just as with Planning Approvals, Building Regulations can be submitted online through the Local Authorities website, once you have made your submission you will be advised of the fees appropriate to your project works.

There will normally be an initial fee for the evaluation of the initial design and then further fees for the on-going site inspections during the course of the works.

WHAT IS REQUIRED TO BE INCLUDED WITHIN A BUILDING REGULATION SUBMISSION?

Simply, the Building Control Officer will be looking for detailed information to understand the scope of the project and to demonstrate that the works will be constructed in accordance with the standards set out in the Building Regulations. The information required will usually consist of:

- Architectural plan layouts
- Structural drawings
- Structural calculations
- Building service design drawings

And

- Material and workmanship specifications (these can be as a series of notes on the project drawings or in a separate specification document).

OBTAINING BUILDING CONTROL APPROVAL

Approval does not stop at the outset of the project. The Building Inspector will continue to monitor the construction of the works throughout the construction phase to ensure that what is actually built on site is compliant.

The Building Inspector will evaluate the scope of the works being undertaken and identify at what periods in the construction phase he will want to undertake his specific inspections. These will normally be around critical periods such as the laying of foundations, installation of roof structures and specific items of installation as well as at completion.

You must make sure you allow the inspector to visit and inspect the works where required before they are covered up otherwise the inspector may request that works are taken down to allow his inspection.

PARTY WALL AGREEMENTS

If your proposed project works are within 6 metres of your neighbour's property then you may find yourself needing to comply with the Party Wall Act.

The Act is detailed and specific about where and when it applies and I would recommend that you take specific advice from your professional advisors on your need to comply and the specific actions that you need to take.

There is a useful Party Wall Explanation Booklet available free of charge from www.communities.gov.uk.

As a general guidance the Act will come into force where:

- 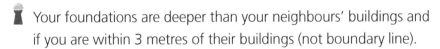 Your foundations are deeper than your neighbours' buildings and if you are within 3 metres of their buildings (not boundary line).
- If you are deeper still and taking a 45 degree line from the bottom of your neighbours foundations and this line strikes your works (including the bottom of your foundations) within 6 metres then you will need to comply.

In such cases you are obliged to notify your neighbour, normally in an exchange of letters detailing the works you are undertaking and providing them with sufficient detail to demonstrate that your works have been appropriately designed not to harm their property. Such proposals may include the foundations of their building structure.

If the neighbour is concerned about your project proposals then they are entitled to hire a qualified structural engineer or surveyor to verify you're design at your cost. It is therefore important for you to make sure that your own structural engineer provides sufficient detail in their design package to mitigate the need for additional work by other parties.

If your neighbour is concerned or opposed to your works (from a structural perspective) then they can cause frustration getting the works started. Ultimately you and your neighbour's surveyors must reach agreement on the structural integrity and provisions but your neighbour cannot prevent you doing the works.

THE PROJECT DESIGN TEAM

THE SKILLS YOU NEED

I have already talked about the skills you need to undertake a project yourself and I make no apology for stating it again here.

To develop and deliver a building project you need a broad range of technical, managerial, administrative, design and physical skills.

It is very rare for even experienced construction professionals to hold all of these skills, which is why you have the different professional and construction specialists, project managers, architects, structural engineers, building services engineers, general builders, plasterers, electricians, plumbers etc. within the industry.

Depending on the type of project and the procurement method you are undertaking you need to consider what the structure of the project team will be. There are three principle areas for this:

- Client / Project Management
- Design
- Construction

When selecting people to work on your project it is essential not only to pick people by their discipline or type of expertise, such as an architect, but you also need to make sure they have the relevant experience in respect of your typical type and style of project.

You have to remember that when the project is completed it will be you, not them, that will be living in it so you have to make sure that whilst they provide the necessary expertise it needs to be directed to meet what you want, not what they want to provide!

HOW TO EMPLOY THE RIGHT PEOPLE

Making sure that you have the right people on board to deliver your project is essential. These are the aspects that you need to look for in identifying potential parties:

Have they got the appropriate technical skills and experience specifically relating to the nature of your project works? It's no good just employing an architect or a structural engineer. You must make sure that they have relevant experience and design flare that matches your specific project needs.

Make sure you get references and follow them up! Take time to get examples of similar projects and check them out. Don't just take the details scan over them and think they look okay and put them in a drawer! Make sure that you at least call the references and discuss their performance with them. Better still actually go out and see what people have had done. In my experience people that have had a great project done love to show them off. Equally, if they have suffered problems and issues they will be happy to air their views. If you get a negative reference though, don't just take it as it is and discount people straight away. Remember, there are always two sides to a story and they might have been impossible clients to work for so if need be check out two or three references. Of course, if there is a consistent trend then you are more likely to have a consistent view! This is so important I have included a specific section on this coming up.

Make sure you **consider your options.** Unless you have strong, specific reasons for why you want to use a particular party always try and **get at least 2 or 3 different parties reviewed** for the services before you appoint someone, especially if you are doing this on your own and don't have previous experience of an individual's work. If you are utilising a project manager then it is likely that they will already know specific parties and will be able to recommend these to you.

Check out their trade and professional body memberships. If they say they are members make sure that their membership is up to date and that the association has no known issues with them. It is also worth checking out if the associations offer any other benefits like backed insurance schemes that you may be able to make use of.

Check out their offices and business address. Make sure you know where they are physically based and where they work from.

TAKING UP REFERENCES

I included a specific section on taking up references because it is so important yet so many people fail to do it either because they are too lazy to do so or they feel uncomfortable about doing it!

Here are some pointers on what to look for and what to do:

Ask providers to provide you a list of references, ideally between 3 and 6.

Make sure that they relate to reasonably recent works say within the last 6 months or so.

Check that the specific people employed on that project are the same people that will be working on your scheme. Like any business they are only as good as the people that actually work for them!

When checking out references get prepared beforehand. Write yourself a questionnaire including the specific aspects that are important to you, include such items as:

- Did they understand your requirements and did they deliver what you wanted?
- Did they provide information in a timely and professional manner?
- Was the information provided in an easy to understand format?
- How good was their communication, were they professional, friendly, and easy to work with?
- How well did they work with other members of the project team?
- How well did they respond to any criticism or issues?
- Did you feel that they added value to your project?
- Do you feel that the service they provided was value for money?
- Would you recommend their services to others?

APPOINTING DESIGN TEAM MEMBERS

There is always a lot of focus placed on making sure that you employ a reliable builder who is not going to run off with your money, but all too often little thought or care is taken about employing the right "professionals" that are going to support your project.

I am called in to pick up many projects around the period when the Planning Application has been submitted or obtained but the client has got to a level of frustration with the architect who as many of the clients say "just does not want to listen to what they want" or is isolated from the project progressing the design in a "cold, hands off" approach from their office. The other issue that comes into play at this point is where the designer only provides their service up to the Planning application service but I will discuss this aspect and in particular the use of "Architectural draughtsmen" later on.

In the meantime, I want to set out some key pointers on how to best appoint professionals to be employed on your project:

Invite potential parties to visit you and discuss your project. Try to establish a feel for:

- Their particular **experience in similar types of project** to what you are considering to undertake
- **How well they communicate** with you, how much they take an interest in what you want. Check their listening skills and ability to re-confirm important aspects back to you
- Look at **how they respect you and your property.** Do they offer to take off their shoes when entering your home? The simple things are often the best indicators!

- What extent they **take notes of the discussion**

- **How interested do they appear** to be in your project? Do they ask searching questions to dig deeper into your requirements, not just the physical works but why you want or need the project, who and how will the space be used?

- **Do they take time to talk you through the project process**, what they believe their involvement will be and **how they can support you and add value?**

Don't be afraid to invite more than one party (not at the same time!) to consider working for you. You need to be able to measure the good from the bad and the best way of doing this is to compare parties against each other.

Always ask them to write back to you following the meeting setting out their proposal and offer in detail. **Never appoint them there and then on the first meeting**. What you should look for when they submit their proposals are:

- A clear **demonstration that they have understood exactly what you are looking for** from your project, not just the basic "to create a rear extension" but how much they go into detail regarding the type of works and are able to re-convey the important aspects you spoke about at the meeting

- **A clearly defined scope of services and a list of outputs** that they will provide as part of their duties on your behalf

- **A detailed, itemised breakdown of their costs**, not just a single figure or worse still a fixed fee % of the construction value. 1), that's just lazy and shows little thought about the specific requirements of your project and 2), if they are getting a fixed % of the construction value where is the incentive for them to make sure the project is delivered in a valued manner offering a fair and reasonable price?

- Make sure that they also set out the services and items not included within their costs. This is a fair and reasonable position to take for items such as dealing with client post tender changes, you may choose to change things which they have no control over which will cost them money to administer, Local Authority fees and other specialist services

- Make sure they provide a clear set of Terms and Conditions of appointment, especially details relating to the timing of payments for their services

- Obtain any additional documents such as a copy of their Professional indemnity Insurance certificate

- Get them to provide a sample package of documents such as drawings and specifications that they have provided for a previous project and will be used as a reference benchmark for the level of detail and content to be produced for your project

TERMS OF AGREEMENT

You must have a clear contractual agreement in place with any party that you employ to provide project services to you, not just the builder with a building contract but also each member of the professional design team. This is often forgotten!

Most companies will usually present their own terms and conditions as part of their formal offer to you, remember that in such cases you have three options:

- You can accept them as they stand
- You can ask for amendments to them, or
- You can present your own terms and conditions

Don't necessarily get sucked in to sticking with their terms if you are uncomfortable with them. Be prepared to say so and be prepared to exclude them if they are not prepared to change if the matters are important to you. Remember, if they are fixed yet you feel you have a fair and valid position then you have to ask yourself "Is this the shape of things to come and how well will they work with you during the project itself?"

Always remember that the Terms and conditions are a Contract. It is a two sided affair and is in place for the benefit of both parties so always make sure that they work for you as well.

Make sure that any Terms and Conditions, supported with the formal offer detail which is part of the "Contract", includes the following clearly defined aspects:

The scope of services to be delivered. Don't be scared to make this detailed with the exact outputs such as a schedule of drawings to be provided, a list of calculations and design details, requirements to attend meetings and provide information.

Delivery dates – Start dates, interim delivery dates, completion dates.

Performance criteria – such as all correspondence and requests for information to be responded to within 5 business days.

Set out costs and payment terms.

Dispute Resolution and Termination Processes. Having this in place is not a sign of distrust; it is just a matter of good professional management to have them in place from the start.

MANAGING THEIR SERVICES

Making sure that your design team ultimately delivers the project solution that you require means that on-going consultation and supervision of their services is required throughout the design stage either by you or your project manager.

The time needed to ensure that this is done properly should not be underestimated and the risk of failing to do this can mean that the project offering slides off track and may take a lot of difficult discussions to get resolved.

It can also cause financial issues and difficulties if a particular member of the design team has been the lead in driving the project in the wrong direction and consequentially means re-work for the other team members. Who pays for this? What impact will this have on the project programme? To what extent is the trust and relationship between the design team members damaged?

The keys to ensuring that the design services are effectively managed are:

Making sure that the project objectives and success criteria are clearly defined and promoted so that everybody involved in the project has a clear understanding of them so they are in no doubt about what is expected not just from them but as a project as a whole. Don't splinter the information only giving individual parties isolated chunks of the information. Let them have a full appreciation of what the common goal is.

Making sure every decision, update and output of information is tested and measured against the project objectives and success criteria. Make this a formal process to ensure compliance and record the review in the project plan. Signing off details can create real power and control.

Speaking out. If you feel the design is deviating away from the project objectives and success criteria you have to shout out and say so, even if you do not understand the detail or the discussions taking place and just want clarification or explanation. It's no good keeping quiet and hoping things will sort themselves out. Frustration will continue to building up inside and you and will ultimately end up disappointment. **Remember people are not mind readers**, you have to tell them. They may not be aware that they are deviating from what you want. It may be that they have been poorly presented with the information during the project briefing or they have naturally reverted back to their own way of doing things without realising. You will gain much more respect from your project team members by speaking up during the design process than waiting until the end and dropping a bomb.

Make sure that **every discussion, meeting and decision is confirmed and recorded in writing and copied to everyone that needs to know.** Don't be scared to copy information to parties not directly involved "for information only" just so it is out there on record. You may find that some aspects will have a knock on effect to other aspects that you had not fully appreciated.

Use pre-defined milestones and events to implement design reviews and sign-offs.

Keep records for everything and keep your project plan up to date. Utilise management tools such as document issue registers, number change requests to keep track and maintain the project risk register.

THE MEMBERS OF THE DESIGN TEAM

YOU, THE CLIENT

Although you may well employ a team around you to deliver your project **never forget that ultimately it is your project and you will always retain certain responsibilities** that you have to deliver and take ownership of.

You have to **be prepared to state what you want** and provide the necessary input of information to receive your required output. It's no good moaning that you don't like the kitchen layout or where the power sockets are located if you have not contributed to the design process or kept quiet when you had the chance to shout out both during the design and the construction period.

You must set the standard for making sure that the works are done in a professional manner. That means proper contract administration, formal letters of appointment and making sure all communication and instructions are issued prior to works being done and are in writing with copies kept on file.

Set and maintain the tone of communication for how people involved in the project work together. Make sure you address people in a clear, polite manner and issue information on time. Always agree dates for them to provide information to you. Just because you have everything in writing does not mean that you cannot strike up a friendly working environment. You can always discuss things verbally; just make sure that it is backed up with written correspondence afterwards.

You need to ensure that you allow sufficient time for both the design stage and the construction of the works. Although pure residential works do not fall within the remit of the Construction Design and Management Regulations directly **you have a legal obligation under duty of care to ensure that you provide the necessary resources (in both time and money) to allow the works to be undertaken in a safe manner.**

Each member of the project team will have responsibilities under their particular contracts and terms of appointment. Remember that each of these contracts have two parties forming the relationship, that means it includes you. **You will have specific contractual responsibilities** such as providing information, allowing access and making payments. Make sure you fully appreciate your obligations under each of these contracts.

THE PROJECT MANAGER

The role of a project manager has been around for a long time in the commercial construction industry but only more recently has it started to develop as a specific role in its own right for residential work.

It's easiest to look at this role as an "Intelligent Client." It's the role and responsibility of the project manager to step into the boots of the client and make sure that the project is delivered in accordance with the client's requirements and in doing so provide the following specific skills and services that the client may not itself hold.

- Technical knowledge and understanding
- Contract management, administration and procurement
- Financial and budgetary planning and control
- Communication and reporting
- Supervision, and
- The time and resources necessary to deliver a successful project

The use of a good project manager can offer clients significant personal benefits over and above the above skills. For clients having the ability to offload all of the stress and running around can allow them to largely step back from the day to day activities and to ultimately enjoy the process and the completed works.

QUANTITY SURVEYORS

The use of a quantity surveyor will not normally be required for a typical domestic project but may be required for a very large scheme or new build. A quantity surveyor is used to construct, identify and measure all the materials, labour and other costs such as storage, hire of equipment; such as scaffolding, and create a detailed project cost plan called a Bill of Quantities.

From the home owners perspective this can be used to get a detailed predicted cost for the works and used as a measure against the procurement process providing a target for the price. It can also add value if you need a better understanding of where the costs are within the project, especially if you need to implement some cost savings.

Builders will also use their own quantity surveyors to price their bids and aid with their own buying activities.

ARCHITECTS AND ARCHITECTURAL DRAUGHTSMEN

The term "Architect" is actually a title that is protected by law in the United Kingdom similar to a doctor or a solicitor. To be able to work as an architect you must have at least seven years training and passed all of the relevant examinations.

Non-qualified or inexperienced providers often trade using the term "Architectural Draughtsmen". Their capability is under scrutiny from the start although it has to be said that there are a lot of very experienced and competent architectural draughtsmen, traditionally these individuals have been involved in the construction industry in some capacity and have CAD (computer aided design) experience. You will often find these people offering services to draw up your plans to Planning application level.

My general experience of this is that they limit their services to this point as it is the relatively easy part of the design to deliver and the real aspects of the design process come at the Building Regulation, detailed design stage.

Therefore there is no guarantee that what they are actually designing will work from a physical construction perspective and if you use this set of Planning drawings for tendering your works you will likely find yourself having to develop the design as you go on site which inevitably means the project costs will increase, the project programme will be delayed and a large amount of stress, frustration and anxiety will be experienced.

THE ARCHITECT, GETTING THE RIGHT ONE FOR YOUR PROJECT

Having the right architect on board to develop your project design is essential if you want the final design to provide your specification for the overall requirements but to also meet the style and feel that fits with your existing home and your personal style.

I think it is fair to say that most people get an architect on board through one of three ways:

- They use the yellow pages, local directories or web site search
- They utilise the local High Street architect, or
- They are recommended by a friend or relative

There is a massive risk in appointing an architect using these methods as I started to refer to at the outset of this section. You don't just want an architect that can design a building structure, you need an architect that is sympathetic to your personal requirements and will deliver a solution that matches your vision and tastes.

Most architects have their own niche or speciality; be it modern, clean designs, visually high impact architectural statements, historic listed buildings, or environmental and sustainable solutions etc. You have to make sure that the architect you work with has the necessary skills, experience and flair aligned with what you desire. You need to make sure that they develop a design solution that meets what you want, not what they do!

STRUCTURAL ENGINEERS

If you are undertaking a project that has specific requirements such as foundations (especially party wall issues), dealing with difficult ground conditions, roof structures and loadings or demolition of structural walls you are well advised to utilise the services of a structural engineer.

Selecting a structural engineer for your project can be a lot harder than appointing an architect as they are mainly used for commercial work and you therefore need to make sure that you identify parties that have the relevant residential experience.

I have come across structural designs many times that have been far too complicated and unnecessary for the project in question down to the fact that the engineer is unfamiliar with residential work on a regular basis. An indicator for this is the use of unnecessary steelwork, especially when designing the structural frames for projects, such as a loft conversion, because they do not have the day to day experience of timber frame. This will inevitably mean an increase in project cost that is unnecessary.

To get the most appropriate structural engineer your best method is to approach your Project manager or Architect to recommend someone. They will often work with structural engineering practices on a regular basis and be in the best position to identify the right party for your specific project needs.

When a structural engineer is appointed you should progress their design process in the same way as the overall project design process.

The first stage will be for them to undertake an option appraisal and sketch scheme design to understand what can be provided and the structural impacts of each solution on the overall construction process, and layout plans. This activity will allow them to identify the particular structural conditions and to identify the alternative solutions open to them. This may, for example, be the choice between a structural frame and a timber solution, the ease in which windows, doorways or other openings can be positioned and the methods of distributing the building loads, which will reflect on the size and type of foundations required.

Make sure that the structural engineer actually visits the site to have a full appreciation of the site, access and construction issues as well as the structural nature of the existing building which will need to be incorporated within the design solution. This may seem a pretty basic and common sense statement but again I have come across situations where the structural engineer has generated their design straight from the architect's drawings. In doing so there is the potential that they will take a lower risk approach to their design such as spanning the loadings across the building from the perimeter walls without making the use of internal load bearing walls. This results in beams being over specified making them larger than necessary and consequently more expensive to the client. There can also be other knock on impacts such as the loss of potential available head height due to the over specification of the structure.

BUILDING SERVICES ENGINEERS

For those not familiar with the role, which are probably most people that are not familiar with the construction industry, building services engineers are responsible for the design of services such as drainage, water services, heating, air conditioning, power, lighting, controls, lifts and other specialist systems such as audio visual.

The use of a build services engineer is traditionally only utilised on commercial or major residential projects. For most small scale extensions and refurbishments the architect will be able to incorporate sufficient design and detail on their drawings and specification of works to allow most builders to be able to develop the final services installation either directly or utilising the skills of their plumbing and electrical sub-contractors.

You have to be aware that an architect in providing their element of design will only be focused on the location of equipment and terminal fittings such as power sockets, light switches and means of lighting etc. Their professional liability will often not cover the building services element and thus the reliance on the design solution will be placed on the builder or even an equipment supplier. It is worthwhile to have someone help you develop the solution specified that meets your requirements not what a salesman wants you to have!

At times the use of a building services engineer can be a worthwhile investment or a necessary service, such instances may include:

 Where you require complex drainage solutions to be incorporated within the project, especially where you are having to deal with limited depth for drainage runs or may have the need for pumping stations and other means of disposal for your waste water

- If you are looking to incorporate specialist design solutions such as high energy efficient or sustainable installations or maybe a solution that forms an important part of the architectural impact of the project that are outside the norm of a typical tradesperson, maybe for example a biomass heating boiler, intelligent lighting control systems, fire detection and alarm solutions, and

- If you have a large service requirement such as multiple bathrooms and you want to ensure that the delivery of water is of a high flow rate and capacity in which case I would get the storage and pipework distribution properly sized

Like selecting the right structural engineer picking a building services engineer for someone not from a construction background can be difficult and I would, therefore, look to your project manager or architect to help you identify and appoint the right party.

INTERIOR DESIGNERS

It is said that **an architect can design your house but an interior designer can create your home!**

Making your space is a very personal experience and needs to be matched to your needs, whilst most people may have thoughts about what they want very few people really have the vision and creativity to understand the potential of a space and how to plan it and dress it to really make it have that wow factor. Employing an interior designer can really be the icing on your cake that makes your project special.

If you are considering using an interior designer as part of your project team I would advise you to **get them involved at the earliest part of the design stage** that you can. Let them work with you and the architect to develop how the space will be used, the layout of fixtures and fittings, where to put storage etc. Don't do what most people do and leave it until the building works have all been finished then get them to come in and just dress the space if you can avoid it; utilise their skills from the start.

STRUCTURING YOUR PROJECT TEAM

When pulling together a team to deliver your project you need to make sure that you have a clearly defined organisation structure, that everybody has a clear understanding of their place within the structure and that their roles and responsibilities are clearly defined, not just in what they are required to deliver to you but also how they interact with the other members of the team and their interrelated responsibilities.

Before you appoint anyone, map out the parties that you require as part of your project both for the design element and for the building works and look to establish a chain of command and communication.

Traditionally this will start with you, the client at the top. Under that you may appoint a project manager to run the project on your behalf. That will be the top tier responsible for defining the high level project requirements and the project control.

Then consider the design team, who will you need on board, an architect, structural engineer, a building services engineer, any specialists? How will each of these be managed? You have various choices here. If you have a Project Manager on board then you may well consider these being appointed on the same level, if not then you may look to appoint the architect to lead the design team and the appointments of the other parties may be through the architect or the architect acts as your representative.

Whilst this is the typical structure you should take account of the scope of the works; understand what is the most dominant part of the project design aspect is and the complimentary skills of the other parties that may be required to deliver the design solution. An example of this may be that the works are mainly a significant structural project involving significant demolition or construction of some load bearing walls, there may be limited if any work to the architectural features or services. In this case the main element will be the structural works and there is minimal need if any for an architect in which case the structural engineer would be most effective in leading the design team. It is really worth thinking about this before diving in and appointing people. If necessary take advice and discuss the project with the potential design team members to help them understand the specific needs of your project and who will provide the most effective leadership.

Finally you will look at the construction team. Again take account of the trades that will be required, building works, ground workers, plumbing, heating, electrical services, kitchen fitters, bathroom fitters, plasterers, landscape gardeners etc. How would you structure them to deliver the works efficiently? We will discuss this aspect later in the builder procurement section.

There are a number of key points to consider when looking how to structure the design, these are:

Single points of responsibility – how much do you want to put single parties in control of the design and the construction elements? **This is largely about transferring the risk** of the works onto someone else. If you do not have a project manager overseeing the works for you may want to look to the architect, for example, to have overall responsibility for the design. You will look to them to take control of the design stage, organise the other design services and make sure that the different design elements all work together.

Time and resource constraints – How much time do you have to apply yourself for co-ordinating all the parties and overseeing the design aspects to make sure that they all work together?

Technical expertise – Do you have sufficient technical knowledge to be able to know that the individual design elements work together and are properly co-ordinated?

Costs – This is always an issue with clients that are not sufficiently experienced in construction. They often see the management costs of appointing either a project manager or an architect to oversee the design stage as an additional unnecessary level of cost to the project. If they actually take time to consider how much time they would otherwise actually have to put into the project and the skills required to effectively manage the project, they would realise the benefits.

GETTING YOUR DESIGN
TEAM TO WORK TOGETHER

Making sure that your design team works effectively is vitally important if you want to develop a complete, co-ordinated design package that allows the project to be constructed efficiently on site by the builder without having to experience design development and changes on site as the project progresses because there are inconsistences between the different aspects of the design packages.

You have to remember that various members of the design team will be involved at different periods and that work done by one party can impact the design works undertaken by others at an earlier stage so you have to be aware of the consequences of sequencing each aspect in the design process.

The keys to making the design team work well are as follows:

 Communicate the design team structure and contact information

 Make sure everyone's contractual appointments are aligned and clearly set out the obligations each party has to the other members of the design team, what information they require

from others, what outputs they need to provide, when to make information available and how to present it

- Circulate all revisions of design drawings and specifications, clearly identifying the revisions that have taken place so they can be considered by each party

- Keep a record of all design development and changes, what has been done, why, and by whom

- Look to have regular project design meetings where all parties attend

- Set out clear design development milestones and sign-off processes **By All Parties**

- Set out how each party can request information from other parties in a controlled process to ensure that it is effectively managed

- All of the above details should be recorded within your Project Plan

LEVELS OF SERVICE AND RISK

As previously mentioned I regularly come across clients (often when picking up projects that have gone wrong) that are or have been reluctant to invest money paying for professional services to either project manage, design or supervise their project works.

They often see this as money that they could be spending on the actual build costs and try to avoid spending this money hoping that they can get by on limited information, putting their trust in the builder to sort it all out for them if it goes wrong.

This is a crazy notion, although good, reputable builders will provide a good service the fact that I am called in to bring projects back on track with such regular frequency demonstrates beyond doubt that trying to cut corners just does not work and that the risks are too high!

It then follows that those clients who have skipped design and management phases have equally tried to take the cheap option when it comes to the building works by not employing reputable, reliable and competent builders! They end up with double the trouble.

Clearly there is not the need to employ a full blown design team for every project. The way to develop the team necessary for your works is to sit down and evaluate the works you are having done and establish the right solution for your project. The simpler that your project is potentially the less detailed design development you will need. Equally, the more complex the requirement the more time and effort you should place on developing the design solution. It may well be that you can break down the various elements of your project, some aspects will be relatively simple but individual aspects will need much greater design development. **The real key to all of this is to make conscious, informed decisions** and not just to be dragged along by the flow or be in a rush to get things done.

DEVELOPING A RISK REGISTER

Utilising a project risk register is an established project management tool that can really add value allowing you to identify, control and focus on the areas of your project that requires particular attention and allowing you and your project team to actively manage the works to mitigate risk on your project.

It may well be that your project is of a fairly simplistic nature but there are certain elements of the works that you may want to pay particular attention to. Equally there may be specific aspects of your project, such as: cost, programme or quality that you really want to manage tightly.

Your project risk register should remain an active document during the delivery of your project, right through to completion.

Here's how to create your Risk Register:

1. Identify the different aspects of the project works to be undertaken. These can be main headings as suggested below and you might want to drive down into these further for specific sub sections (i.e. demolition may cover different parts of the structure, site clearance and, asbestos removal).

a. Demolition

b. Clearing the sites

c. Foundations

d. Main Structure

e. Roof

f. Staircases

g. Windows

h. Building Services etc.

2. Next, create a new column and list what the specific risks of these may be, you may want to consider elements such as cost certainty, programme, quality, disruption to neighbours, site health & safety, site security, etc.

3. Then in the next column provide your own descriptive text as to what the issues may be, i.e. buying bespoke kitchen may have a long delivery time that could impact on the project programme

4. The next thing to do is to consider the frequency of the event, how likely you think the risk is. Give it a score of 1-5, 1 being very unlikely and 5 being very likely

5. Then score the impact of the event happening, again giving a score of 1-5. 1 being not an issue to 5 causing major problems to the project.

6. Then in the next column create a risk score by multiplying the frequency score by the impact score. This will allow you to identify the real priorities that need to be addressed.

7. Once you have this create a new column titled "Management Plan" then for each item state how you intend to manage the risk. It may be for example, making sure that the bespoke kitchen is ordered by a certain date and has defined contractual terms to be delivered by a certain date. It may well be that if the risk cannot be managed then you revert to an "off the shelf kitchen" that can be obtained more easily. Obviously the lower

the risk level the less you may need to define the management plan. Low level items may not even need considering if the level of risk is acceptable. That judgement and decision is down to you.

8. Finally create a last column that is titled "Status" then against each item give it a traffic light status:
   a. Green-Closed, Risk Gone
   b. Amber Risk Management Plan Implemented, On Track
   c. Red, Risk Management plan Not Yet Implemented

The most important aspects of this process are that **you identify your project risks at an early stage** and **you make informed conscious decisions** about how they will be addressed and **you manage this process throughout the life of your project,** right up until completion.

PROJECT RISK REGISTER

ASPECT	RISK TYPE	DEFINED RISK	FREQUENCY (1 unlikely - 5 likely)	IMPACT (Severity of Failure on Project Success)	RISK SCORE Frequency x Impact	MANAGEMENT PLAN How the risk will be managed	STATUS
Demolition	Cost	Scope of works to be tendered figure in cost plan developed through standard rates.	1	3	3	Works have been procured and are within the cost plan budget	Closed
			only need to procure once.	*Over budget could cause the project overall to be over budget*		*Risk mitigated.*	
	Programme	Anticipated 6 weeks. Construction not due to start for 12 weeks so no immedaite problem	1	1	1	No serious risk. No specific management required. Demolition contractor has prepared demolition programme indicating 5 weeks.	Closed
				There is plenty of float ion the programme so little impact		*Risk mitigated*	
	Quality	Using approved demolition contractor. Not final build so minimal risk.	1	1	1	No serious risk. No specific management required.	Plan Implemented
			Demolition will only take place once	*does not contribute to the final construction so negligable impact*		*Risk minimal but works still to be completed.*	
	Disruption	Road closures will be required to remove debris from site	5	1	5	Formal Method statements to be submitted by contractor detailing management process and agreed times and dates with local authority	Plan Not Yet implemented
			A large number of removals from site will be required so this has a high frequency	*will not effect final construction*		*Plan for raod closures not yet agreed.*	
	Health & Safety	Demolition works are hazardous therefore significant control required.	5	4	20	Demolition contractor to be pre-evaluated as suitable by CDM Co-ordinator. Detailed method Statements to be prepared for each elememnt of the demolition works to ensure effective planning, control and supervision of the works. Site supervision to be maintained at all times during the demolition works.	Plan Not Yet implemented
			This will incorporate a lot of activity with H&S management	*The H&S consequecies can be significant if not well managed*		*Demolition contractor evaluated. Detailed method statements in preparation.*	

MANAGING
THE PROJECT
FINANCES

SETTING YOUR PROJECT BUDGET

The must do part of determining your project objectives is to establish your project budget. There are two directions from which this can be generated and it is ultimately a mixture of both that will come together to give you your budget:

 Determine what you can afford to spend, and

 Determine what works, what you want and how much that will cost.

Obviously, the choice between the two will be dependent on what your drivers are; what is most important to you, cost or quality or even programme (time)?

Developing your initial project budget should be done as part of your own initial research. Break down each aspect of what you are looking to achieve and try and establish outline costs against them. You may find it useful to put bands of costs against certain aspects that may have some flexibility, such as the quality of the kitchen fittings to be used, to test the boundaries of your budget and the extent of its flexibility. This will allow you to understand how achievable the works are and allow you to identify the areas where compromises and decisions will need to be made.

There are plenty of places where you can obtain indicative cost information as part of your research including construction books, magazines and a host of websites. Be aware though that many of the websites that ask you to sign up and lead on to you being inundated with builders and suppliers trying to get your business. You can get your project manager or architect to prepare this cost information for you and help develop your budget right from the start.

PREPARING A SCHEDULE OF COSTS

This is easiest prepared on an excel spread sheet and is worthwhile presenting in a format that follows the project programme so that you can identify the project cash flow and payment stages to give you a full appreciation of the payment periods.

Down the left hand side I would schedule out all the different financial aspects that you will need to incorporate, my suggested headings are as follows but these will of course be dependent on the nature of your particular project.

PROFESSIONAL SERVICES

- Client time (this is the cost for your personal time!)
- Project Manager
- Architect
- Quantity Surveyor
- Structural Engineer
- Building Services Engineer

 Interior Designer

 Other

STATUTORY APPROVALS

 Planning Approval

 Building control

 Party Wall

CONSTRUCTION

 Preliminaries

 Site clearance

 Demolition

 Ground works

 Utility Connections

 Walls

 Doors & windows

 Roof structure

 Joiners

 Drainage

 Plumbing

 Water services

 Heating

 Power

- Lighting
- Sanitary Fittings
- Kitchen Fittings
- Appliances
- Decoration
- Floor finishes

OCCUPATION FIT-OUT

- Fixtures and fittings
- Furniture

ANCILLARY COSTS

- Relocation and removals
- Storage
- General expenses
- Home insurance
- Borrowing fees & bank charges

PROJECT CONTINGENCY

These items can then be broken down further, in the second column, into sub headings to allow a more detailed price breakdown, for example Kitchen Fittings may include individual elements such as the main carcases, doors, worktops, handles &

fittings and equipment such as the sink, fridges, freezers, extracts etc.

In a third column you should then record comments in respect of how you have established the cost. It might be on a measured rate, from a quotation provided by a supplier, or even a guessed budget.

In the fourth column state what type of cost this is:

- A Fixed Cost/Price
- An Estimate
- Provisional Sum

In the Fifth Column you might want to record a potential range for the works that you can consider for financial planning purposes.

The finally in the sixth column record your project budget figure. This will be the target figure that you intend to spend on each element and if you add these up down the page you will have your total project budget.

Across the spread sheet you may then want to set out the project programme and put these costs into a cash flow to give you a clearer understanding of when the expenditure for the project will stake place.

If you can also add an income stream against this if you are obtaining funds along the construction process.

Project No
Contract
Client

Project Address
Client Name

the residential
Project Manager

Procurement Package	Ref	ELEMENT	SUB ELEMENT	Status	Cost	VAT	Total	Invoiced to Date	Outstanding to be Instructed exc VAT	Outstanding to be Instructed inc VAT
		CONSULTANCY SERVICES								
			Project Management	Instructed	£ 3,425.00	£ 685.00	£ 4,110.00	£ 1,200.00	£ 2,225.00	£ 2,670.00
			Architectural Planning Design	Instructed	£ 850.00	£ 170.00	£ 1,020.00	£ 850.00	£ -	£ -
			Architects Building Reg Design	Fee Agreed	£ 700.00	£ 140.00	£ 840.00	£ -	£ 700.00	£ 840.00
			Structural Design	Fee Agreed	£ 300.00	£ 60.00	£ 360.00	£ -	£ 300.00	£ 360.00
					£ 5,275.00	£ 1,055.00	£ 6,330.00	£ -	£ 5,275.00	£ 6,330.00
		STATUTORY APPROVALS								
			Planning Approval	Estimate	£ 172.00	£ 34.40	£ 206.40	£ 172.00	£ -	£ -
			Ordinance Survey Plan	Estimate	£ 75.00	£ 15.00	£ 90.00	£ 75.00	£ -	£ -
			Building Regulations	Provisional Sum	£ 1,100.00	£ 220.00	£ 1,320.00	£ -	£ 1,100.00	£ 1,320.00
			Party Wall Agreement	Assumed not required TBC	£ 800.00	£ 160.00	£ 960.00	£ -	£ 800.00	£ 960.00
					£ 2,147.00	£ 429.40	£ 2,576.40	£ -	£ 2,147.00	£ 2,576.00
		CONSTRUCTION								
		Building Works	Prelims	Provisional Sum	£ 4,200.00	£ 840.00	£ 5,040.00	£ -	£ 4,200.00	£ 5,040.00
			Demolition	Quotation	£ 3,200.00	£ 640.00	£ 3,840.00	£ -	£ 3,200.00	£ 3,840.00
			Groundworks - Foundations	Quotation	£ 2,400.00	£ 480.00	£ 2,880.00	£ -	£ 2,400.00	£ 2,880.00
		Ground Floor	Main Building Works	Estimate	£ 21,547.50	£ 4,309.50	£ 25,857.00	£ -	£ 21,547.50	£ 25,857.00
			Windows & doors	Provisional Sum	£ 850.00	£ 170.00	£ 1,020.00	£ -	£ 850.00	£ 1,020.00
			Kitchen Units	Provisional Sum	£ 15,000.00	£ 3,000.00	£ 18,000.00	£ -	£ 15,000.00	£ 18,000.00
			Kitchen Appliances	Provisional Sum	£ 2,200.00	£ 440.00	£ 2,640.00	£ -	£ 2,200.00	£ 2,640.00
			Decoration	Provisional Sum	£ 800.00	£ 160.00	£ 960.00	£ -	£ 800.00	£ 960.00
			Flooring	Provisional Sum	£ 900.00	£ 180.00	£ 1,080.00	£ -	£ 900.00	£ 1,080.00
					£ 41,297.50	£ 8,259.50	£ 49,557.00	£ -	£ 41,297.50	£ 49,557.00
		1st Floor	Main Building Works	Estimate	£ 15,210.00	£ 3,042.00	£ 18,252.00	£ -	£ 15,210.00	£ 18,252.00
			Windows & doors	Provisional Sum	£ 850.00	£ 170.00	£ 1,020.00	£ -	£ 850.00	£ 1,020.00
			Sanitary Fittings	Provisional Sum	£ 600.00	£ 120.00	£ 720.00	£ -	£ 600.00	£ 720.00
			Bedroom 1 Wardrobes	Provisional Sum	£ 400.00	£ 80.00	£ 480.00	£ -	£ 400.00	£ 480.00
			Decoration	Provisional Sum	£ 800.00	£ 160.00	£ 960.00	£ -	£ 800.00	£ 960.00
			Flooring	Provisional Sum	£ 630.00	£ 126.00	£ 756.00	£ -	£ 630.00	£ 756.00
					£ 18,490.00	£ 3,698.00	£ 22,188.00	£ -	£ 18,490.00	£ 22,188.00
		Additional Works	Roof	Estimate	£ 8,000.00	£ 1,600.00	£ 9,600.00	£ -	£ 8,000.00	£ 9,600.00
					£ 8,000.00	£ 1,600.00	£ 9,600.00	£ -	£ 8,000.00	£ 9,600.00
		PROJECT TOTAL			£ 67,787.50	£13,557.50	£ 81,345.00	£ -	£ 67,787.50	£ 81,345.00
				TOTAL	£ 75,209.50	£15,041.90	£ 90,251.40	£ -	£ 75,209.50	£ 90,251.40

PROVISIONAL SUMS

These are budget items where the actual cost is not known at the outset and a budget figure has been placed in the overall project budget plan A typical example for this may be the cost of the kitchen fittings which have not yet been specified and priced for.

The budget plan will therefore have an allowance; let's say £18,000 as a provisional sum for the kitchen. As the design is developed and the kitchen gets specified and the price is fixed then the provisional sum item is instructed for the actual cost, say £16,500.

A saving against the project budget will then be made. Don't forget that an item may ultimately come in over the provisional sum which will mean the project budget will go up!

The important factors relating to the management of provisional sums are:

Make sure that the provisional sum budget estimate at the start is realistic. If the overall project budget is not working because it is too expensive don't try to artificially hide that fact within the provisional sums in the hope that it will all sort itself out along the way. You are bound to be disappointed.

Be careful how you present these sums to outsiders, especially suppliers and builders who are involved in pricing these elements at a later date. You are almost giving them a top level number against which to price against. My advice would be to present the pricing document and project budget without the costs included.

Manage the release of provisional sums in the same way you administer a formal contract variation. Get the scope clearly determined, get the prices and any impact to the programme presented by the builder or supplier and then once you have all information raise a formal instruction. Once it has been instructed then you can include it on the project financial reporting.

Don't try and hide non related elements within a provisional sum item. If a cost item gets missed or another element of the works comes in over budget and you need to find additional costs to meet it elsewhere in the project budget don't fall into the trap of trying to include it elsewhere. Keep your project budget plan true. If costs don't come in as you want it's no good attempting to fiddle the books or kid yourself. You need to maintain clarity and understanding of the financial situation. You should not plan to underspend on the provisional sums in order to bring the overall project budget in line due to cost issues elsewhere! Remember all your decisions need to be taken consciously and consistently in alignment with your overall objectives for the project.

PROJECT CONTINGENCIES

This is a budgetary allowance to cover unforeseen elements or items coming in over budget. Essentially **it is a financial safety net for your project.**

The amount that you place in your project budget plan as a contingency will largely depend on the certainty of the works. The following will therefore all contribute to the amount of contingency you allow for:

The nature of the works. Are they relatively simple and easy to perform? Is there much to go wrong?

The level of design detail. How clear and well defined are the works? Is the builder able to price it accurately? How much design development will be undertaken during the construction?

The condition and knowledge of the existing site. How much knowledge do you have of what lies 'behind the walls' of your site? Do you know what you will find when you start stripping out ceilings? You might come across asbestos. Where you thought all the walls were sound the plaster might start falling off and you have to get more of the walls re-plastered than originally expected! The electrical wiring may be found to be in a poor condition and a re-wire is needed.

The nature of the Building Contract. What level of risk has been passed on to the builder?

Quotations and pricing. Do you have firm quotations and fixed prices for goods and materials?

How well developed, detailed and utilised your project management tools are. Are you using them consistently throughout the project? Is your project budget sufficiently detailed? Is your risk register well developed and have you implemented the management plans to reduce or mitigate the risks? Do you carefully manage change control procedures, avoiding verbal unrecorded instructions on site?

The effect of outside influences. Things such as delays due to bad weather, supplier non-performance, changes in interest rates and borrowing costs.

The value you should place in the project contingency will largely be a personal feel based on the above considerations, or through taking the advice from your project team. As a guideline, for a well-defined project, I would suggest an allowance of 10% of the construction value and for a poorly defined project maybe 15 or even 20%.

CONTRACT PRELIM COSTS

Prelims are the cost items that the builder incurs relating to his own site establishment and control of the works. Typical items that are included within this cost are as follows:

- Mobilisation costs
- Site establishment such as toilets, security, health & safety protective wear
- Project insurances
- Equipment hire
- Waste disposal, and
- Administration overheads and supervision costs

These costs can either be identified as a fixed lump sum or a fixed weekly cost. Remember that if there is an extension in the project programme due to project changes then the contract prelim costs are likely to go up as a result of the change.

RETENTIONS

Retentions are nominated sums, usually a fixed percentage of the works that are retained or held back during the course of the project and at handover to cover the costs and provide the builder an incentive to provide all of the necessary documentation, project manuals and certificates on completion, to address any snagging items and to deal with any project defect during the warranty period.

They are common place in most building contracts although most builders, particularly in the residential business are not particularly keen on them.

The level of retention will be dependent on the scale and nature of the works but I would normally suggest a retention of 2.5% of which 1% is paid once the project documentation is handed over and all the snagging is completed and then the final 1.5% paid at the end of the defects liability period (the set time, normally around 3-6 months after the completion of the works where the builder is still responsible for undertaking and repairs or making good) period and the final project handover is completed.

ESTABLISHING A PROJECT ACCOUNT

It is recommended that the client establishes an interest-bearing joint account in the names of the client and the principle builder for the construction works element and maintains sufficient funds in it throughout the term of the project to pay the value of the works.

This is a standard principle and found in most Building Contracts. It provides confidence to the builder that the funds are available for their payment, given that they are undertaking the works in advance.

Once the payment approval process is expedited then the monies relating to the valuation can be removed by the builder through a cheque process that requires signature by both parties.

At the end of the contract any monies left remaining in the account will be refunded back to the client.

WHEN TO PAY THE BUILDER

You should only pay the builder when they have completed specific elements of work.

NEVER PAY THE BUILDER IN ADVANCE! I cannot over emphasise this. It is probably the most common failure that I see from projects that have gone wrong and where clients have lost money.

If builders ask for money before they have started work or asking for advance payments during the course of the works then this should immediately ring alarm bells that something is not right. You might get the arguments, he has got to pay his men or his suppliers or his sub-contractors but don't listen to them and stick to your guns.

Terms for payment should be clearly defined within the Building Contract and you should stick to them.

Any reputable builder will have the necessary trade accounts with their suppliers so they should ever have to expend monies in advance.

The only exception to this may be if you are having a specialist, bespoke item provided for your project and the supplier requires an up-front payment, in which case I would recommend that you either purchase this directly yourself and supply it to the builder for installation or you get sufficient evidence from the supplier to demonstrate that the order is made in your name and you own the rights to that item.

PHASED OR STAGED PAYMENTS

Depending on the nature and size of your project you will either pay in a single final payment, if your project is relatively small, or if it is something that is going take more than a month it is likely that you will make a series of phased payments as the project progresses.

It is best for you to be in control of this and to set out the payment schedule within your tender proposal document. More detail on this can be found in the specific section later in the book.

My advice on this would however be **not to make this a calendar payment** (i.e. every two weeks or monthly) **but to make this based on the phased or staged completion of works elements.**

There are specific reasons for this:

You can easily define and agree elements of works are complete and to the necessary quality. It is difficult to access works that are only half done.

You can directly relate payments back to the priced schedule within their tender.

It gives the builder motivation to complete elements or work rather than letting him start lots of elements but never finishing them.

You may want to incorporate elements for "beneficial use" i.e. you may want to start using defined areas of work, maybe a kitchen, prior to the whole project being completed. If this is your plan make sure that it is identified as a requirement in the Building Contract and you have split out the pricing elements accordingly in the tender invite package.

THE PAYMENT PROCESS

The payment process needs to be formally set out within the Building Contract so there is a clear procedure and mechanism to prevent unexpected demands for costs. The Building Contract will also determine the specific timescales appropriate for each stage of the process and the format that each notice must be presented in.

The process should consist of the following clear steps:

1. At the agreed time as set out in the Building Contract the builder shall issue a payment valuation. This should clearly set out the overall project value, the detail of works completed at the time of the valuation, consequently the value of the works completed to date and then deductions for the payments made to date. This will then give you the value of that application. You should make sure that the overall project value details variations and provisional sums elements that have been instructed so you have a complete up to date appreciation of the project costs and there is total clarity of the project finances between both parties.

2. On receipt of the valuation you (or your project manager) will have an agreed number of days to review the valuation and agree that the works are satisfactorily completed to the extent that the builder is presenting.

3. Having reviewed the valuation if you do not agree with the valuation then you (or your project manager) must inform the builder accordingly and advise them of the items in dispute. These can either be jointly reviewed and an agreement reached or as a minimum you can advise the builder the sum you will make payment for at that point if the dispute is on-going. Be clear here that you cannot unreasonably withhold payment.

4. Once the valuation sum has been agreed the builder will submit his format application for payment (invoice) to you.

5. If you are utilising the services of a project manager then they will receive this and once satisfied will issue you with a certificate for payment, simply signing off that it is now appropriate to release the funds.

In addition to the payment process the Building Contract will provide dispute resolution processes, these are dealt with later in the book.

PAYING THE BUILDER

As discussed earlier the most effective manner for paying the builder is through the utilisation of a dedicated project bank account that requires the signatures of both the client and the builder to release the funds.

Payment can be done through a cheque or on-line bank transfer. The most important aspects to making the payment are:

You must have a clearly pre-presented application for payment and **you must make it clear exactly what any payment is for**. This will stop the builder requesting payment for the same element of works twice!

Utilise 3rd party electronic records of the payment. It is always good to be able to call up bank records to demonstrate payments, should disputes arise. Make sure that if you are paying by cheque then write on the back of your cheque the invoice / application number or similarly if doing an on-line payment write these details in the reference box option.

Always get a receipt for payments from the builder and again make sure that these receipts clearly cover what the work was for (i.e. application no 3, invoice XXX), the date the payment was made and the method of payment.

Never hand over post-dated cheques to the builder at the start of the works. If they ask for them then alarm bells should be sounding very loudly.

Never pay in cash. Builders often ask for this but my advice is to always say no. You will have no evidence that the payment has been made and you can easily fall foul of demands and disputes over payment.

Builders will sometimes suggest that you will be able to get works cheaper by not having to pay tax. You must be aware that there is only tax relief for builders on New Build Housing works so this is unlikely to apply to your works and secondly they do not have to be registered for tax if their turnover is around £80,000 (depending on the current HMRC levels) therefore this is just not true! Again alarm bells should be ringing!

MANAGING CHANGE

The failure to effectively manage the change process is one of the most common reasons clients end up with project costs escalating out of control or suddenly receive a nasty unexpected bill from their builder at the end of the project. As well as the financial impacts, delays to the project programme (timescales) are also a common problem.

The Change process must be formally detailed within the Building Contract, identifying roles and responsibilities in respect of the process and timescales. It must be adhered to!

Changes will occur on most projects, especially where works are being done to an existing building and issues only become apparent when you start undertaking the demolition or breaking out walls, floors or ceilings.

Similarly, whilst detailed designs are developed, once things start being constructed sometimes the use of space may want to be reconsidered and power sockets, light switches and other features may feel better in slightly different locations. These will need to be managed through a controlled change process.

Change is not a bad thing as long as it is done in a controlled manner. It is all a part of the building process and ultimately the success of the project will be getting the right solution. What is important is to make sure that and change is properly administered. Both you the client and the Builder have to be disciplined in this respect. I would be happy if the builder says he is not doing any change without an instruction. This is not being negative it is being professional. This is how it should be done:

1. **Never give a verbal instruction for a change.** By all means discuss changes with the builder on site but still revert to the formal change process.

2. **Set out the change request requirement in writing**. Make these requests sequentially numbered so that everyone involved knows that they have a complete set. Ideally a formal Change Request Form should be used for the project. You need to identify what it is you want to change, why you want it and why it is needed. This can be very useful to keep your focus in alignment with your vision for your project. The change request may be supported with revised design drawings and specifications or other relevant technical details issued "for information only".

3. Issue it to the builder in the format agreed within the contract. Remember **that if different providers are involved that it is also issued to them as well as it may have wider consequences** than you initially appreciate, so they will need to opportunity to consider as well. At this point this is not considered an instruction. **Remember that changes must comply with the Building Regulations and any planning or Party Wall Agreements.** If necessary revised applications will need to be submitted.

4. On receipt the builder should consider the request. There may be an element of discussion with you or the design team to develop the requirement, especially if they identify aspects that need to be addressed or have significant consequences. Remember to keep a record of these discussions.

5. Once the detail of the change has been agreed then **the builder should formally respond setting out the detail of the change, the cost impact of the change and the effect to the programme of the change.**

6. Having received this you can decide if you want to formally instruct the change or not. If you do then you should **issue a formal change instruction detailing out the agreed works, the cost and the programme impacts**. This change should be **accompanied with format variations of the drawings and specifications and a revised project budget as required**.

THE BUILDING
CONTRACT

DO I NEED A BUILDING CONTRACT?

I am still shocked how many times clients ask me if they really need a building contract. I consistently get called in to sort out projects that are not going well only to find out that there is not a formal building contract in place!

It does not matter how simple or low value your project is, it is still a legal transaction that needs to be delivered in the right way. You do have natural protection from contract law in the fact that you have an agreement with the builder to construct something in return for financial payment and that they should carry out the works competently.

There is all sort of advice out there. I have even read other construction books suggesting that a contract is not necessary but this is because people fail to appreciate the benefits of the contract, they perceive it as a stick to stop being ripped off, rather than a tool to effectively manage the works. They see the need for a contract as a sign of a lack of trust between the parties instead of recognising it as just being professional!

A contract is not there just to protect the client; it is there to benefit both parties. The builder gets benefit from it as well, so there should be no need for them to be negative about having a contract in place.

Think of the following benefits that a contract provides:

- **A clearly defined framework** identifying the specific roles and obligations of each party

- **How the works will be carried out.** Remember works are being done on your home, often while you are still in occupation therefore you need to have a say on how the builder behaves, how he protects your property and maintains a safe environment, what hours he works etc. Don't forget that the benefits work both ways. If you stipulate the working hours then you need to make the site available to him at that time. You cannot suddenly decide to have a lay in one morning and deny the builder access, compromising his ability to meet the programme completion date.

- **How and when the payments are made**, so there are no awkward and stressful moments when the builder suddenly demands money.

- **How to manage change** and keeping control of the project finances

- **It also sets out the mechanisms for what to do when things go wrong.**

136

CONTRACT TYPES

There are two common types of building contract that can be utilised, a traditional contract and a design and build contract.

The traditional contract sets out the works to be undertaken in detail and the builder constructs to the design and specification that he is provided with. This contract requires a much greater detail of design to be provided by the client and the design team but allows the flexibility of the client to implement changes as the project progresses. Under this form of contract the client retains the financial risk and is required to pay the builder the actual construction cost.

The **design and build** option consists of the client providing the builder with an output style specification, i.e. sets out what they want the builder to develop and the builder delivers this but takes on the design responsibility, often including the selection of materials and methods on construction. Obviously the output specification can be very high level or quite detailed. It may well be that the project is only specified in detail for particularly important aspects that the client wants to retain particular control over. The benefit of this form of contract is that the financial risks are passed onto the builder who provides a fixed price for the works. In this case the client has to accept that the builder will price in a risk factor into his costs and it is difficult for the client to implement any changes once the contract has been signed.

The type of contract used is up to the client, based on their desire to control various aspects of the project, such as: cost certainty, level of specification and the ability to influence the design during the construction process.

CONTRACT STRUCTURE

The contract needs to be simple and easy to understand and use. It needs to be set out in a manner that can be easily referenced covering each of the areas in defined sections with the necessary cross referencing to related sections where appropriate.

Too often, off the shelf contracts can be disjointed and require substantial cross referencing so if you are using one of these and preparing it yourself make sure that you have a thorough run through to make sure all aspects are covered.

Principally your contract should include the following sections; these will be addressed in detail through the following sections of this book.

- The front-cover titling of the project
- Summary of the key aspects
- The Contract execution, where the contract is signed
- The responsibilities of both parties
- The description of the works
- Financial control

- Project insurances
- The project programme
- Defects liability period
- Management of the site
- Sub-Contracting
- Terminating the contract
- Dealing with disputes
- Schedule of documents

THE CONTRACT CONDITIONS

One thing that is often missing from contracts is a simple section at the start outlining the overall intention of the project and the terms of the contract. This can be a very helpful element to give an appreciation of how the contract sits in relation to the works and the project team and what are the expectations and basis of the Contract.

The key aspects of this summary are:

The Contract Intent – This basically sets out that the contract is between the two parties; what design information including specifications and drawings are provided, what the builder may have to provide within his own design obligations and any specific issues important to the project that the builder needs to be aware of, such items may include specific Planning Approval Issues, Building Regulation requirements, plus any access restrictions or critical conditions that will impact on the manner that the works are undertaken.

The Relationship of the Parties – This sets out the project structure i.e. the contract is between the two parties, the nomination of any agent and any residual obligations in respect of the design team or other nominated suppliers or contractors.

Summary of the Works – Provide an overview of what the project works are; what is required to be delivered, specific aspects relating to the specification and specific project objectives or any other relevant information that the builder should be aware of.

Financial management – Summarise how the works will be instructed i.e. under a single instruction or multiple orders for different elements of the works.

The Project Programme – Identify the headline dates applicable to the works including the start date, end date, phased completion or other critical milestones such as established dates for any specific activities that need to be carefully planned for such as the breaking through into the occupied areas, stripping out the kitchen, isolation of the heating, delivery of critical equipment and materials or any other relevant event.

THE RESPONSIBILITIES OF BOTH PARTIES

Remember that a Contract is a defined legal relationship between two parties and as such both you as the client and the builder have obligations, which each party requires the other to meet.

RESPONSIBILITIES OF THE CLIENT

The following are traditionally the obligations that you as the client will typically be expected to provide under the Contract:

Responsibility for the Documents: You are required to make sure that the information you provide (generally prepared on your behalf by your design team) are fit for purpose, i.e. will work and comply with the appropriate standards meeting all legal requirements including Planning and Building Regulations.

Payment of Fees: You must pay all relevant fees including Planning and Building Control Fees.

Obtain Permissions: As Client, you must obtain all necessary permissions (Planning, Building Regulations and Party Wall) before the builder starts work and keep your requirements to any conditions relating to the approvals throughout the course of the project. Note that if you breach the conditions of these permissions you must pay the builder any losses and damages that they may suffer as a direct result of rectifying works to fall in line with these permissions.

Pay the Builder: You must pay the builder in full and in a timely manner in accordance with the conditions within the Contract.

RESPONSIBILITIES OF THE BUILDER

The typical obligations that apply to the builder will include the following:

Carry out the Works: The builder will deliver the required works with reasonable care and skill and to a reasonable standard.

Deliver in a Timely Manner: To complete the works in accordance with the defined programme dates.

Comply with Permissions and Approvals: To deliver the works in accordance with the Planning applications and Building regulations and the approved design and specification.

Undertake the works in a Compliant Manner and in Accordance with the Contract Conditions: To manage the works and to operate the site in line with the requirements set out in the contract.

Provide the Necessary Documentation: To provide all guarantees, test certificates, warranties and insurances that apply to the works.

Be responsible for the works: Including all works within their contractual responsibility delivered directly or utilising sub-contracted or novated suppliers.

THE DESCRIPTION OF THE WORKS

The scope of the project works will be provided through a package of information provided by the client to the builder. This will normally be formed of the following elements:

WORKMANSHIP SPECIFICATION

This is normally a text document prepared by the various members of the design team comprising of the following aspects:

Particulars: These incorporate the design requirements, material specifications and output requirements that need to be met.

Workmanship: These are the installation standards, how the work is to be installed and the techniques, materials and methods to be used. These may be specific details i.e. not pouring concrete below a minimum air temperature which will prevent it from curing.

DRAWINGS

These consist of plan layouts, elevations and specific details identifying the works to be performed. They will be notated with supporting information that can include elements of the supporting notes and specifications.

If you procure the works through different packages you need to make sure that the works required under each package are clearly defined.

SPECIAL DESIGN PACKAGES

In addition to the main project designs there may also be specialist areas of works that have their own sets of specifications and drawings. Typical aspects that may fall under this category can include:

- Fitted kitchens
- Audio-visual technology solution
- CCTV and security systems
- Landscape designs

FINANCIAL CONTROL

This section sets out the contractual processes for how and when payments are to be requested and made to the builder. Typical aspects included in this section of the contract include:

IF INTERIM PAYMENTS APPLY

Usually for projects over 28 days it is normal to make interim (staged) payments. Remember, never pay the builder in advance and only pay the builder for the value of the works undertaken at the time of the valuation.

THE APPLICATION AND PAYMENT PROCESS

This will cover how the builder submits requests for payments and what they can include in respect of completed works; materials on site etc.

The Defined Timescales: Set out when valuation requests can be made either staged based or at an agreed time frequency such as monthly and the timescales for the client to review and approve the requests.

- **The Formal Invoice**: How this is raised and submitted
- **Payment:** By the Client
- **Deductions:** For any Retention

FINAL PAYMENT PROCESS

Set out how the builder will present the final valuation for the works incorporating the base scope of works, all changes, variations, release of provisional sums and contingencies.

Agree the verification and sign off process and the release of funds. Don't forget to deal with the retentions.

WITHHOLDING PAYMENT

If you do not agree with the valuation final account, this section of the Contract sets out how you must deal with the situation in a formal manner providing sufficient information and detail to the builder as to your specific objections and issues.

INTEREST

If you (the client) fail to pay the amount due to the builder in the timescales defined within the contract then you must pay interest against the unpaid sums to the level determined within the Contract.

TRANSFERRING CLIENT RIGHTS TO INSURANCE MONEY OR LOCAL AUTHORITY GRANTS

If all or parts of the works are funded through these external funders then the Contract should allow necessary provision for the benefits of these funding rights to be transferred to them.

USE OF A JOINT PROJECT ACCOUNT

I would recommend that an interest-bearing account is set up for the project in joint names between you as the client and the builder. This offers clear availability of the funds and ring fences the funds for specific use against the project. This is common practice in many projects.

The Contract will usually require you to pay in an agreed % of the project value at the outset of the project and keep this topped up in line with the overall project cash flow.

You will be required to pay the builder from this account. I would avoid making payments in any other manner as it will complicate the financial management and should disputes arise regarding payments paying from one account provides great transparency.

At the end of the project if funds are left, including any interest acquired, this will revert back to you the client.

MATERIALS AND GOODS

Set out the obligations on the builder to provide materials. Typical obligations will include:

- To provide new, unless specifically agreed
- Of satisfactory quality
- Of the description the client (design team specification) gives
- Compliant with appropriate Standards and Codes of Practices in force at the date of placing the order

- Fit for the purpose that they are intended
- To provide the materials and equipment in a reasonable timescale
- You, the client will be responsible for the quality, compliance and fitness for purpose of any materials and equipment that you provide to the builder to install

WHO OWNS MATERIALS AND GOODS?

You will not own any materials and goods delivered to site until the builder has been paid for them.

CHANGING THE WORKS

The Building Contract must include a formal change process which must be adhered to. Failure to maintain discipline in instructing change is the main way project costs spiral out of control and people end up with massive unexpected bills during or at the end of a project.

The key elements of the change process that should be included within the Contract are as follows:

- There must be a defined method by which the client can request a change. This should always be in writing, never allow a verbal instruction to be contractual
- An obligation for the builder to provide a detailed impact of the change and get them to confirm back the detail of the change including any consequential impacts; the financial change to the contract and any impact to the programme.

- Set timescales for each party to respond to their obligations in the change process

- A written agreement formally instructing the change (until such time the change has not been instructed). The written instruction should confirm the date of instruction, the change to be incorporated, agreement of the variation of the contract sum and project programme if applicable.

THIRD PARTY CHANGE REQUESTS

There may be times when changes are driven by the requirements of a third party such as the Building Control Officer. I would recommend that the same Change process is utilised to administer the variation in a similar manner.

UNEXPECTED WORK

It is inevitable, especially working on existing property that some unexpected works will arise. Often, it is only when you start stripping out ceilings and walls that you find additional works items that need to be addressed. This is where your project contingency should come in to play.

In such cases again I would recommend that the Change Process is applied used to instruct and control these aspects.

USING THE BUILDERS EMPLOYEES, SUB-CONTRACTORS AND TRADESMEN

As the client you should not use these people to undertake any additional works outside of the Contractual Provisions. The Builder is fully entitled to charge for these services and elements that you may have thought as being done as a "favour" can suddenly appear as an unexpected expense at the next project valuation. If you want anyone to undertake additional work or services for you, then instruct them under the formal change process.

LABOUR-ONLY SERVICES

The Building Contract will allow provision for where you may provide materials and goods and the builder is employed in a service only role to install them. This may include receiving receipt and even the collection and transportation of the goods.

DELAY OR DISRUPTION

If the works are delayed or last longer than expected and this is not at the fault of the builder then the builder has the right to increase his price. If it is your fault as the client then the builder will be entitled to claim for any losses and expenses caused. It is worth including some element of provision in the Building Contract from the start such as "the Builder will allow for 3 days of delay due to bad weather within the Contract price".

PROJECT INSURANCES

INSURANCE BACKED GUARANTEES

The Builder may provide an insurance backed guarantee for his works under a structural warrantee or through a trade scheme. If you are having significant structural works done then this is worth considering.

RESPONSIBILITY FOR LOSS AND DAMAGE

Your obligation as the Client – will be to ensure your insurances provide cover for the existing structures and contents; for any loss of or damage to them, unless this falls within the builders works obligations.

You must notify your insurers of the works, maintain adequate insurance through the course of the works and provide evidence of the insurance that is in place.

The Builders obligations – the builder will be responsible for existing structures and contents if the loss or damage is caused by the builder's negligence or by the negligence of any person the builder is responsible for. If only part of the damage is caused by the builder then they will only be liable for their element.

The builder will be responsible for insuring against any loss or damage relating to the project works until practical completion has been reached or the client has terminated the agreement.

If the builder is taking on an element of design or specification then the builder will be required to take out suitable insurance cover for this element and maintain these insurances until the end of the project, during which time any legal action could be pursued.

The builder must maintain adequate insurance through the course of the works and provide evidence of the insurance that is in place.

LIABILITY FOR PERSONAL INJURY

The builder will be required to pay the client any losses or damages as a result of your legal liability for personal injury or death caused by the works or activities undertaken by the builder.

You as the Client will be responsible for personal injury or death caused by your negligence or any person you are responsible for.

LIABILITY OR DAMAGE TO ANY PROPERTY OR ANOTHER PERSON

The builder will be liable for any losses or damages resulting from the works and activities that they are responsible for in the execution of the works.

THE CLIENT AS AN INSURED PERSON

Normally the builder will include the Client as an insured person under the Builders insurances.

NOTIFICATION OF CLAIMS

You or the builder must notify insurers immediately about any claims and operate to comply with the terms of the insurances to prevent them from becoming invalid.

THE PROJECT PROGRAMME

SETTING THE PROJECT PROGRAMME CRITICAL DATES

Once the project procurement has been completed you should agree the project programme and critical dates with the builder. This will include the Start Date, the Completion Date and any specific phased dates, project milestones or specific activities that have a fixed time associated with them which require setting within the Building Contract.

In setting the start date, you as the client must ensure that you will be able to execute your obligations such as clearing the site and removing furniture and equipment. To aid this it is worth including a clause within the Building Contract requiring the builder to provide you with a written list of actions that they require you to address prior to the start date. This list should be issued to you to action at least 5 working days prior to the start date.

EXTENDING THE CONTRACT PERIOD

The terms under which you the client will reasonably extend the Contract Period will be set out, these usually include the following:

- Delayed or lack of instruction by the client
- If the builder suspends all or part of the builders obligations under the conditions in which he is entitled to do so
- If the project is obstructed by any other matter that the builder does not have control of
- Weather conditions
- Civil commotion, wars, riots and lock-outs

DEFECTS LIABILITY PERIOD

The defects liability period is a set period of time following the completion of the works at handover, during which the builder retains a responsibility to deal with any defect that arises due to faulty workmanship or materials (unless these were provided by the client).

In such cases the builder will not be responsible for:

- Defects due to the condition of the site or relevant property that existed before the builder began their works, as long as the builder considers the condition of the site and writes and notifies the client. In such cases the builder will have carried out their duty by giving the client warning. If the client insists that the builder should proceed the builder should confirm that the item remains at the client risk

- If the condition of the site could not reasonably have been expected before the works started
- Defects caused by the client or any other party

MANAGEMENT OF THE SITE

This is a really important section of the Contract yet rarely gets the attention and detailed input that it requires. This is the section of the Contract where you have the opportunity to identify and stipulate how the builder will conduct his work on site. Remember, this is your home and the works will impact for at least a short period of time on how you live and how your family operates, so make sure that any details that are important to you are included in sufficient detail.

Make sure that you discuss and agree these with the builder during the tender procurement process and that they are incorporated within the final executed contract document.

Here are some of the key points worth considering and incorporating within the Contract:

ACCESS TO THE SITE

As the client you must allow adequate access to the site and keep this clear and free of obstructions to allow the builder to effectively carry out the works in a safe and secure manner. Take time to think what the best way of gaining access is, remember that this may change during different phases of the project as the works develop.

Ideally the means of access should avoid regular access through the on-going living areas of your property.

CLIENT PROVIDED SERVICES

The builder is likely to need at least water and electricity to allow him to undertake his works. Set out in the Building Contract where these supplies are to be taken from. The builder should then allow, within his costs, for establishing temporary supplies that will enable him to undertake the works with on-going minimal disruption to you. Generally, utilities are provided to the builder at nil cost but make sure that you stipulate this, or if you intend to charge for these you must set out how they will be charged in the contract. If you are paying for these then it is in your best interests to make sure that the builder operates and uses supplies efficiently and does not cause unnecessary waste.

STORAGE OF MATERIALS

Set out an agreed location that the builder can use for the storage of materials. I would also recommend that you require all tools and equipment to be removed from site every night and that the storage of materials and equipment is kept to a minimum. In agreeing space make sure that you consider the security impact; that the location is out of view to outsiders and does not encourage or attract potential burglars.

You will also want to state that any goods, materials and equipment are held on site at the builders risk while the works are undertaken. You should consider the insurance implications and appreciate when such materials and goods have been paid for and therefore become your liability.

MANAGEMENT OF RUBBISH AND WASTE

Clearly define how the builder shall manage waste, especially if they need skips located on site. The key point to include is that the site is kept in a clean and tidy at the start and during the course of the works. This means that all rubbish is to be removed from site on a regular basis and not allowed to excessively build up. The builder is also responsible for the disposal of waste for his works and those of sub-contractors and tradesmen working on his behalf.

It is a common problem for the builder not to be around when his sub- contractors are on site and the client ends up having to clear away their rubbish. Kitchen fitters are a typical example of this, so this is something you may need to actively manage with the builder if you don't want to be shifting rubbish from your site.

WELFARE FACILITIES

I would generally recommend that your Building Contract states that the builder will provide their own welfare facilities for toilet accommodation, washing etc. Do not allow them to use your facilities.

SITE PROTECTION

The builder should provide security hoardings, fences alarms and other protection necessary to provide a safe and secure site and protection to your home.

You will need to agree a protocol for managing any alarm systems at the property, consider when they will need to be isolated, who holds codes and who is responsible for setting the alarms at the end of each day. Are you prepared to let them have codes or is your system sufficiently flexible to allow different users to have their own codes, in which case you can at least interrogate who turned alarms off in the event of an incident etc. Ideally do not let anyone have codes except for the security system engineer... and change the codes regularly.

Keys are also an issue. Again, try and keep the phasing of the works separate from your normal living area and plan the works so the period of any open access to the house is kept to an absolute minimum. Don't hand over keys unless you absolutely have to, and even then hand these over at the start of the day and make sure the builder hands them back each evening before leaving for home. Do not allow the builder to take your keys off site.

TEMPORARY SERVICES

Make sure your Building Contract sets out that the builder is to provide, within the contract sum, all necessary temporary services (heating, water, drainage and electrics) and means of access to allow you to have continued reasonable occupation of the property during the course of the works, if you are remaining on site while the project is carried out.

MEANS OF PROTECTION

The Contract should include for the builder to provide all necessary means of protection to your property, internally and externally, and also protect any neighbouring property if applicable to avoid damage of the existing or newly constructed structures, fixtures, fittings, finishes and landscaping.

Any damage that does occur should be made good by the builder at his cost.

HOURS OF WORKING

The Contract should clearly set out the hours that the builder can work on the site. These should be defined for weekdays, Monday-Friday, Saturday, Sunday and Bank Holidays.

It is no good leaving these open. Make sure you properly define them but remember once you have stipulated them you cannot prevent access to the builder without being in breach of contract and then you become open to a potential claim.

LIMITS ON HOW THE SITE CAN BE USED

You may wish to stipulate specific conditions that are important to you and how the builder and his operatives should conduct themselves on site. It is worth asking your builder if they have their own company policies or Code of Conduct as to how they operate their business and the standards that they expect from their employees, sub-contractors and suppliers.

Typical conditions include:

The Use of Radios: Are you happy for them to use them, if so how loud? The use of radios is often frowned upon but actually can help maintain a good environment for the operatives on site. It keeps them happy and most importantly working hard and as long as it does not compromise health and safety and your own enjoyment of the home it may not be a problem.

Smoking: This should not be allowed and expressly prohibited in the Building Contract.

Dress Code: Suitable overalls, work cloths and uniforms should be worn at all times. A shirt must be worn at all times.

Language and behaviour: Remind the builder that they are working in your house and therefore they shall behave in an appropriate manner.

Parking: The builder shall not park vehicles on the premises and will be responsible for the parking of their vehicles. Short term access may be provided only for the delivery and unloading of goods and materials.

CLEARING THE SITE ON COMPLETION

Before the Completion Date the builder must remove all rubble, surplus materials, rubbish, tools, scaffolding and protection, leaving the site in a clean and tidy condition making good any damage to finishes including landscape.

SUB-CONTRACTING

The builder is unlikely to hold the full range of trades and skills directly within his business as it is not economical for him to retain specialist trades that he is unable to provide full time work for. In such cases he will look to sub-contract these services out.

Typical services that may be subcontracted are as follows:

- Brick Layers
- Plasterers
- Carpenters
- Plumbers
- Electricians
- Kitchen Fitters

As part of the builder's tender submission you should get the builder to identify the aspects that will be sub-contracted out. If the sub-contracted works are important to the project you may want to consider paying particular attention to that aspect of the due diligence of the builder's performance, and if necessary get references for the sub-contractor as well.

Generally the builder can use a sub-contractor for any element of the works but the builder will still be responsible for the works undertaken and therefore the sub-contractor's performance.

The client can nominate specific sub-contractors that you may require the builder to use however they have the right to validate the sub-contractor themselves and may require the client to retain the liability for the sub-contractor's services. If this is the case any such conditions will need to be defined in the contract.

TERMINATING THE CONTRACT

There may be reasons why the Building Contract needs to be terminated either through circumstance or performance. Your Contract should provide clearly prescribed ways in which this can be affected but don't forget that there may be liabilities or consequences in doing so.

YOU'RE RIGHT AS THE CLIENT TO TERMINATE

You should construct the contract to allow you to terminate without affecting your other legal rights and remedies. You may end a Contract in one or more of the following circumstances:

- Without reasonable cause the builder has:
    - Stopped work for 14 days in a row
    - Failed to deliver the works with steady progress
    - Or if you as the client have issued a written notice to the builder telling them to re-start work or work with steady progress and the builder does not do this within a set stipulated period, usually 7 days from the notice
- If the builder financially or as a business entity cannot trade effectively
- If the builder becomes bankrupt
- If the builder goes into liquidation

- If the builder makes an arrangement with the creditors
- The builder is wound up
- If a receiver or manager is appointed over the Contract

Note that the builder can still use their legal rights and the other provisions set out within the Contract to resolve the issue.

THE BUILDERS RIGHT TO SUSPEND OR TERMINATE THE CONTRACT

Remember, the Building Contract is an agreement between two parties and as such the builder has similar rights to protect his business. These are the sort of terms in place that the builder has to rely upon.

Without affecting their legal rights and remedies the builder can end all or part-suspend all or part of their requirements for one or more of the usual conditions:

- If you, the client fail to pay any amount due and still fail to pay after a prescriptive time set in the Contract, usually 7 days, after they have given written warning demanding payment and advising that they intend to suspend all or part of their obligations
- If you, the client or anyone you employ interfere with or obstruct the works or fail to make the site available to the builder (without good reason) for the contract period. As previously identified you need to make sure that you are fully aware of your responsibilities when stipulating the working hours. If you know prior to the Contract being let that you are

going to be away on holiday for example for a couple of weeks during the works you can stipulate in the Contract that no works will take place during this period should you wish

- If you, the client become bankrupt or go into liquidation and are unable to pay for the works
- If you cause or attempt to cause the withdrawal of a grant or insurance payment the rights of which have been transferred to the builder

BUILDER RIGHTS TO RECOVERY

If after the builder has suspended or terminated the Contract be aware that he still retains the rights to all relevant payments as well as any reasonable costs and reasonable losses he has suffered (including loss of profit).

Equally, you as the client can use your similar legal rights and the other provisions set out within the Contract to resolve the issue.

DEALING WITH DISPUTES

If a dispute arises between you and your builder the Contract should be prepared to provide a set of clear methods to remedy the situation in a professional manner rather than a bitter dispute breaking out and the builder sending round a couple of heavies demanding money.

These are the principle methods that can be put in place:

Conciliation: Both you, the client, and the builder can work together to agree an amicable way forward. If the builder is a member of a professional trade association, and if you are using this book, then they will often have insurances in place as part of their membership scheme that will appoint a third party to facilitate this process.

Adjudication: This method allows either you or the builder to refer disputes to an adjudication party, who will be members of a recognised body familiar with the industry. They will hear each side's position and make a judgement and a remedy to be put in place.

Court Proceedings: Parties can take action through the County Court up to the small claims limit or through full County Court proceedings.

Arbitration: Either you, as the client, or the builder can refer the dispute to arbitration. In such cases you will mutually agree who will hear the dispute. The builder's trade association may appoint an arbiter on your behalf. Arbitration will be carried out under the Arbitration Act 1996 Construction Industry Model Arbitration Rules 1998.

SCHEDULE OF DOCUMENTS

The Contract should include a schedule of all associated documents which form part of the Contractual Agreement.

These will include:

- Copy of any Planning Consents and conditions that apply
- Copy of the Building Regulation Notices and any conditions that apply

- Project drawings including architectural, structural, building services and any other design details
- Specifications and schedules of works
  - Performance and workmanship specifications
- Detailed estimates, quotations and pricing schedules
- Any other documents
  - Building insurance certificates
  - Party Wall licences

Remember that these are all as much Contractual Documents as the main written Building Contract.

SCHEDULE OF NAMED SUPPLIERS

If you have specific requirements for the provision of equipment, systems, materials and even elements of the installation works then you can name these within the Contract.

Typical nominated suppliers may include:

- Bathroom and Kitchen Suppliers
- Audio-visual systems
- Art work and other bespoke equipment

SCHEDULE OF BUILDERS NAMED
SUB CONTRACTORS

As previously identified the builder may choose to sub-contract elements of the works. These should be identified and named within the Building Contract.

FINDING
THE BUILDER

HOW TO FIND THE RIGHT BUILDER

Making sure that you find the right builder is essential in delivering a successful project and is one of the biggest worries most people have when undertaking a project.

This section aims to take you through the right steps to identify, validate and finally select the right builder(s) for your project.

Initially there are a number of ways of identifying potential builders to work on your project. A few of these are listed as follows:

- Get recommendations from friends and family that have had work done themselves
- Look out for builders doing works locally in your area
- Check with Trade Associations
- Speak to your local Trade Suppliers
- Ask professional practices such as architects and project managers for recommendations

The ways to avoid finding your builder include:

- Taking names straight out of the phone directories
- Builders making doorstep approaches

Initially I would look to get a long list of say 6 builders to undertake the next stage of detailed due diligence and verification.

UNDERTAKING DUE DILIGENCE

INFORMATION GATHERING

Once you have your long-list then you should do some research and validation of the building companies.

Set out a questionnaire or document to collect consistent, comparable data on each of the parties then ether arrange to meet them or speak to them on the telephone to introduce yourself and arrange for them to provide the following information:

 Basic Company Information

- Trading Name

- Business Address

- Contact Information

- Name of Business Owners

Description of Projects and Services that they undertake. Make sure that they are compatible both in type of work and size of project that you are having done and geographical location

- Membership Details of Trade Associations that they belong to
- Obtain at least 3 reference projects of similar works to yours that they have completed over the last 6 months and ideally one that is currently on site

How well they respond to your requests will be an important part of the validation period as well as the details they give you. It will give an early indication as to how well their business systems are set up, how good their communication is and how interested they are to do your project 'legally' and correctly.

Don't be afraid to ask the builder questions, including if this is the sort of work that they are interested in undertaking!

CHECKING THE INFORMATION

No matter how good the information they provide appears to be make sure that you validate it to check that it is current and true. Ask questions!

Check out their company registration details. I have come across a number of builders that have been employed on projects that have gone wrong and I have been called in to sort out only to find that the builder is not even registered with Company's House let alone any trade association! Nowadays it is so easy to check this sort of information out on the internet so there is no excuse not to do it.

Have a look at their trading address. Again, this only takes a couple of minutes on the internet and you can get photographic views of their property. Do they appear to be based where they say they are? If they have trading premises do they look reputable, in existence for a long period of time etc?

Follow up Trade Association Memberships. Are they current? What level of membership do they have? Are there any on-going disputes or issues under investigation? Are they covered by any insurance schemes run by the association?

Follow Up References. I find it happens time and time again where people have put in the effort to obtain references but never bothered to follow them up. Firstly, make sure that they are genuine and, as with the advice I gave for the design team members earlier in this book, take the time to go and see the works that they have undertaken and speak to people. I say it again, people who have had great works done love to show them off, similarly if the builders have let them down and not performed then they are equally keen to see that others do not fall foul of the same problems.

Create your own check list of questions and areas to cover. Typical things that you may want to include are:

- Did they have a proper Building Contract?
- Did they stick to the terms of the Contract?
- Did they deliver the works that were specified?
- Did they deliver to a good quality?
- Were there defects at the end of the project and if so how quickly did they get these resolved?
- Were there any post completion defects and if so how well did they respond?
- Did they stick to the programme timescales?
- How well organised were they at managing the project finances?

- Did they request payment as agreed?

- Did they try to add extras over and above the scope of works?

- How good was their communication, did they keep you up to date with progress?

- How well did they respond to questions when you asked them to explain things?

- How reliable were their sub-contractors?

- Did they manage their sub-contractors well?

- Did they keep the site tidy and have respect for your home?

- Do you think that they offered value for money?

- Would you use them again?

MEETING THEM

If you feel that following the validation process the builders appear good candidates for your project then it is worth meeting them face to face before the tenders are issued.

The objectives for this meeting are as follows:

- To decide whether you like them? Do you think you will be happy for them to be working on your home?

- To give them the opportunity to clarify any issues raised during the validation process

- To give them an introduction to the proposed project, re-confirm that they are still interested

🔦 To talk through the likely project programme to make sure that they have the resource and capacity to undertake the works when you want

PROCURING
THE WORKS

TENDER OR NEGOTIATE

Deciding how and when you procure the works will largely depend on how much you want the builder or supplier to be involved in the design process and how much design responsibility you want them to take on.

If your builder is working with you to develop the design then you will be looking to negotiate the cost of the works with them. I would recommend that in such cases, before you start employing the builder, that you at least agree a schedule of hourly rates chargeable for different trades such as general builder, labourer, bricklayer, plasterer, plumber, electrician and the mark-up costs normally as a % of costs for materials and hiring of equipment so you have a basis as to how the costs will be built up, and to construct and evaluate these as the design and construction progresses.

If you have the design largely developed and you are looking for more cost certainty then the tendering route is more favourable.

HOW MANY BIDDERS?

I would normally recommend that you look to obtain alternative bids from 3 or possibly 4 builders for larger projects.

Tendering of works can at times be frowned upon by some builders who naturally prefer to be in the position of sole bidder without competition. It will be important for you to be able to generate a good list of diverse builders that may not regularly compete for work against each other.

There are views and stories of builders getting together to pick and choose the works between them before submitting their bids. Whilst to a limited degree this might happen I do not believe it as frequent as some people seem to suggest and is often put around by builders to open the door for them to negotiate works.

One issue that the typical home owner does have is that they are only likely to undertake this type of project maybe once in 20 years, which means from the builder's perspective the project offers no particular long-term value to them.

Utilising the skills of a Project Manager who is regularly going to tender with projects on behalf of their clients brings this bulk buying power into play. Builders become more interested and serious about presenting a competitive bid as well as being more responsive to the delivery of works on site when they know that it has potential to be part of an on-going work stream if they successfully deliver the project.

THE TENDER PROCESS

PREPARING A TENDER INVITE

A formal tender invite pack should be issued to the builders bidding for the works. This pack should include the following elements:

- The invite letter
- The Building Contract
- The Pricing / Payment Schedule
- Builders Method Statement Template

THE INVITE LETTER

This should be a formal letter inviting the builder to submit a bid for the project works. The letter should set out who the invite is issued on behalf of, what is included within the tender pack, what needs to be completed, when the bid needs to be returned by and where it should be returned to.

The letter should also detail any specific requirements of the bid process such as how to submit queries, requests for clarification and details for arranging inspections of the site.

You will also want to include a non-collusion clause stating that they must not discuss any elements of the bid with other builders bidding for the work.

THE CONTRACT

The draft Contract should be included, completed in as much detail as possible, setting out the terms and conditions including restrictions under which the builder will be required to carry out the works.

There will be certain aspects that cannot be completed until the Contract is awarded such as the start and completion dates although these can be indicated as draft dates for the bidding purpose.

THE PRICING / PAYMENT SCHEDULE

Set out the pricing document based on the individual elements of the works that are to be undertaken. Take time to consider how this is best set out to co-ordinate with the validation of phased or stage payments depending on the nature of the works.

Typical stage payments can include:

- Site Clearance
- Ground works

- Main build structure element
- Structure and roof watertight
- Plastered out
- Services first fit
- Finished and second fit of services
- Decoration
- Landscape and externals

BUILDERS METHOD STATEMENT

The builder should be encouraged to set out how he proposes to deliver the works. The level and detail to which this section is completed will give you a good feel as to the extent they have considered and understood the works to be delivered, the conditions placed against them within the Building Contract and overall how interested and committed they are to the project.

It will also allow you to have a better appreciation of how the works will be delivered and any considerations that you have to be aware of.

THE TENDER PERIOD

For most tenders I would allow a 4 week tender period from issue of the tender to receipt of the tender bids.

Prior to issuing the tender package I would recommend that you speak to the builders to make sure that they are still interested in submitting a bid and advising them of the tender dates. This will greatly reduce the risk of builders not returning tender offers and compromising the procurement process.

Once the tenders have been returned, depending on the level of queries, clarifications and the level of detail submitted within the submissions, I would normally allow a 2 week period for tender evaluations to be completed and to be in a position to appoint your preferred builder.

BIDDER SITE INSPECTION

During the tender process you should allow each of the bidding builders the opportunity to visit the site so they can fully appreciate the works involved, consider conditions that they will have to work under and evaluate how they will deliver the works.

You should allow this visit to be undertaken during the second week of the tender period. This will give the builders the first week to review the tender documents, understand the works to be delivered and to draw up a list of issues to consider and discuss when they are on site. It will then allow them 2 weeks to prepare the pricing and methodology for the tender submission.

You should allow all bidders to attend the site on the same day but **not** at the same time. Make sure you allow sufficient time between each visit to prevent them bumping into each other.

The visits should be conducted in a formal manner. Initially run through introductions of the people in attendance, check that they have received all of the tender documentation and then allow them to inspect the site. Once this has been completed there should be an opportunity for them to ask questions and get any clarifications. I would recommend that your project manager chairs the visit. If you have not appointed one you can either do this yourself or get a lead member of your design team to do it.

Do your best to address any queries but if you are not sure then agree to respond after you have taken advice from your design team.

To make sure that all of the bidding builders submit their bids on the same basis you should take notes of any additional information or points you have discussed with each of the bidders and issue a note of all the items to all of the bidders so they all work to the same information.

WHAT ELSE TO LOOK FOR DURING THE SITE INSPECTION

The Site inspection is an important part of the procurement basis as it offers a good opportunity for you to evaluate the builder in action. Consider it a mini interview process.

Here are some key points to look for during the inspections:

- **What is their communication like?** Did they confirm attendance in advance? Were they friendly and did you feel comfortable with them in your home?
- **Did they act in a professional manner?** Were they polite, well behaved and respectful?
- **How interested did they appear to be in the project?** Were they knowledgeable about the scope of works, had they taken time to review the documents? Were they taking measurements

and taking time to think about how the project would be executed?

🗼 **Did they appear technically competent?** Did they know what they were looking at? Did they point out key issues and suggest that they had a good understanding as to how they intended to undertake the works?

🗼 **Were they looking for items of extra works from the start?** Did they appear to have a sharp commercial angle?

THE TENDER RETURN

Tender offers should be returned fully in accordance with the requirements of the tender invite and on time, using the required document formats completed in a clear and well-presented manner.

This will be an immediate indicator that they are serious about working on the project and how reliable their business processes are.

If individual bidders fail to provide the necessary detail in their returns then you need to seriously consider their ability or desire for the works.

DEALING WITH TENDER CLARIFICATIONS

You should allow the builders to be able to submit queries and clarifications relating to the tender documentation.

You can allow this through email but make sure that any details or possible variations are fully recorded and where possible noted for discussion and inclusion within the final Building Contract.

As previously stated you should allow all bidders to be provided with any additional information or clarifications to ensure that all bids are submitted against a consistent set of requirements.

ALTERNATIVE PROPOSALS

To provide a clear baseline for evaluation of the bids I would recommend that each bidder submits their base offer in full compliance with the Contract and design, issued in the tender package, and incorporating any specific issues issued to all parties during the clarification process.

It may well be that the builders are able to offer you alternative specifications or solutions that may be of benefit either through ease of delivery, reduced programme periods, cost savings or a combination of all three.

In such cases you do not want to miss these opportunities therefore you should allow the builders to submit alternative proposals in addition to their base bid for consideration.

This will also be a good indicator to see which builders have fully considered the scope of works and are able to offer practical opportunities. Be careful however, they may also have other motives such as better discounts with certain suppliers where you may not necessarily get the full financial benefits. For example, they may not have specific capabilities thus looking for alternative approaches for works that they cannot deliver to the original specification etc.

TENDER INTERVIEWS

Having evaluated the tender returns you are likely to have a preferred potential bidder or maybe it is close between the top two bids and you remain uncertain who to appoint.

Prior to instruction it is worth meeting at least the preferred bidder to run through their proposal to make sure that everything evaluated is correct and is fully compliant.

At this interview make sure that you have the person that has prepared the bid on behalf of the builder and also the person that the builder will be placing in charge of the project present, as you will want to make sure that they are competent and you are happy to work with as they have a crucial role in the success of the project.

EXECUTING THE CONTRACT

Once all the details of the procurement are closed out the final version of the Building contract should be completed and signed by both parties.

Make sure that each party has a signed copy and keep a third copy in a secure location.

You are now ready to go!

CONTROLLING
THE WORKS
ON SITE

THE PRE-START MEETING

Making sure that the project works get off to a well organised and positive start on site is very important because it sets the tone of how the works will be delivered and establishes the relationships between the people involved.

There is nothing worse than the start date arriving only for the builders not to turn up or works not commencing because the site has not been cleared, materials and equipment have not arrived, lack of access because you cannot find keys etc. It puts everyone on the back foot; it generates immediate frustration and instils a lack of trust between project team members.

That is why it is so important to hold a formal pre-start meeting in advance of the commencement of works on site. This is not just the builder popping round for a coffee to say hello and tell you what day he will be starting!

There needs to be formal structure to the meeting. It needs to have a clear start time and held at a location where people can sit round a table and make notes. Your dining room is fine; it doesn't need to be a meeting room or anything formal like that, but does need to be a place where the parties are able to discuss the items without significant distraction or interruption. If you have employed one, your Project manager should organise and chair the meeting or you could ask your architect to do it if you are uncomfortable running it yourself.

WHEN TO HOLD THE PRE-START MEETING

Ideally the meeting should take place approximately two weeks prior to the works commencing on site however if there are significant issues that have an immediate effect on the project programme, that need action sooner rather than later, then you may want to bring this meeting forward or even have a pre-pre-start meeting to address the specific issues.

Make sure that you notify the parties in sufficient time and send a copy of the agenda. They may wish to add other agenda items to be included in the meeting.

WHO SHOULD ATTEND THE PRE-START MEETING?

Obviously the client and the Project Manager and the builder will need to be there. Make sure that the builder brings along the individual who will physically be managing and responsible for controlling the works on site if it is not him directly.

You may wish to bring in the architect or even the structural engineer if the works are of a specific nature that they will have a significant input.

WHAT NEEDS TO BE DISCUSSED AT THE PRE-START MEETING?

There needs to be a clearly set out agenda for the meeting. I would recommend that the following agenda items are included but this should be adapted to meet your specific project requirements.

- **Introduction of the people involved.** Identify the roles and responsibilities of everyone involved and make sure that you generate a project contact list with names, emails and phone numbers

- **Commercial status.** Make sure that the contract(s) have been fully executed (signed) and there are no outstanding contractual issues

- **Overall project programme.** Run through the key project dates including the start date, any interim key milestones such as defined dates for disruptive works, major deliveries, project milestones, phased completions and the final completion date

- **Outstanding information.** The project should have an 'information required register' where if any party has a query or requires input from another member of the project team then this should be recorded and reviewed on a regular basis to ensure the items are addressed and do not cause project delays

- **Review the project risk register.** Make sure that any items that have an impact on the project programme are addressed

- **Site preparation activities.** Run through what activities need to be completed prior to the start date. This may include clearing away furniture and other client property, completing the condition survey, getting licences for a skip and getting that ordered, arranging sets of keys, making sure your insurers are notified etc.

Site establishment activities. Agreeing what the builder will put in place for the operation of the site such as temporary toilets, security fencing, temporary power and water supplies, creating a storage area.

Agreeing the activities for the first day. Make sure there is a clear understanding of exactly what will happen on day one. This might not be much or it might be a lot, but it is always best to have this understood and agreed before the day. The builder may just be planning to do the site establishment for example and will only be on site for a few hours. That's fine if that is all that is planned but if not discussed imagine how the dissatisfied the client will feel if the builder turns up for a couple of hours then leaves site.

Agree that activities for the first week (or possibly two). As above make sure that there is a clear understanding of what will be going on. It is likely to be quite a hectic period particularly if there are aspects of demolition and removal of rubble or the digging of foundations. Particularly, discuss details of disruptive works, such as turning the power and water off, which may have an effect on your living within the house.

Confirm emergency arrangements. In the event of incidents who will respond? What if power is lost to the home or there is a water leak or there is a break-in to the site? Who do you call and who does what?

Agree the date of the next meeting. Always make sure you agree the frequency of the progress meetings and the time and date of the next one. It is useful to try and keep them at a regular point, i.e. every Thursday afternoon at 2pm.

RECORD KEEPING AND ADMINISTRATION

A formal record of the meeting needs to be kept in meeting notes. Make sure that the action points are clearly identified, together with the dates that they need to be addressed and that the person responsible for them is identified. Circulate them to all the attendees and any other party that needs to have a copy, in a timely manner, so they have adequate time to address the actions.

UNDERTAKING A SCHEDULE OF CONDITION

If damage to your home is identified during the works, arguments and frustration and even full blown anger can occur as a dispute arises and questions are asked as to who caused it and was it there before the works even started etc. It is something that happens all too often and can bring down the relationships of everyone involved in the project.

In order to prevent this, I would recommend that a full site inspection is carried out prior to the commencement of the works; not just of the construction area but of the entire property and surrounding grounds. I would even recommend doing an inspection of your neighbour's property if appropriate.

The inspection should be done by the client or your project manager and the builder. Make sure that it is done in good daylight.

The inspection should be formally recorded with a schedule of existing defects and also a comprehensive set of photographs, recording not only the defects but also the full condition, including decorative level. With digital photography this is very easy to do so there should really be no excuse not to do this.

Once the defects schedule and register of photographs has been completed both the client and the builder should sign it and hold their own copies. A third signed copy should be held in the project plan. You may want to issue a copy to your neighbour at least containing their relevant and get them to sign it off as well for record purposes.

THIS INSPECTION MUST BE DONE BEFORE ANY WORKS COMMENCE ON SITE

This will provide a valuable point of reference should any claims regarding damage occurring during the project.

RISK AND INCIDENT PLANNING

When having works done on your home there is always a risk that an incident may occur such as a water leak or loss of power or even a possible break-in.

Too often there is little planning put in place to address this in advance of the event, on most domestic projects, but just a few simple plans can make what will be a distressing event more manageable and less stressful to all parties involved.

Here are some tips on how to plan ahead:

Identify and label main points of isolation for the water mains; hot and cold water services, incoming electrical power and distribution boards and gas supplies. It would even be helpful to have these marked on a drawing so if someone unfamiliar with your home turns up to deal with an emergency you can point them in the right direction.

Make sure you have the contact numbers for the builder and some of his key staff including both office and mobile numbers so they can be contacted 24 hours a day if needed.

Consider incorporating response times within their contract. This is probably overkill for a residential project but if the project is large enough you might want to consider it.

Make sure that the site itself is well managed; tools, equipment and especially ladders are stored in a secure location or removed from site overnight, goods and materials are secured and not held in bulk on site for long periods before installation and all keys are securely locked away in a key cupboard etc.

Make sure that means of escape action plans are thought about and talked through with your family. Remember your possible secondary means of escape from your house may be a building site. Can you use this route? Is it kept clear or do the works or equipment obstruct it? Just think about it in case you need to exit your house quickly and cannot use the main exit.

PROGRESS MEETINGS

Regular progress meetings should take place to ensure that the project is being delivered as planned, remaining on track financially and to programme timescales. They provide a formal opportunity for the parties involved on the project to provide updates and address any potential issues to ensure the successful completion of the project.

WHEN TO HOLD PROGRESS MEETINGS

During the main activities on site I would look to hold them on a regular basis, ideally weekly or fortnightly. Try and keep to a regular day and time such as 2pm every Thursday so people can plan for them in their own schedules.

You may choose to adjust the frequency during periods when works are quiet, there is not a lot happening on the project plan and there are no significant aspects such as outstanding information or project risks to be addressed and the works are on budget and programme. Just because things are going well though does not mean that you should take your eye of the ball and let things drift.

WHO SHOULD ATTEND?

As with the pre-start meeting you and/or your project manager should be there together with the builder. Other parties should attend determined by the on-going site activities and the works that are coming up and need planning for. It may be that the kitchen installer, for example, should attend as the kitchen is being installed in a couple of weeks' time and it is the right time for them to be introduced to the site to ensure the specific planning for their activities is undertaken in a timely manner.

WHAT SHOULD THE FORMAT AND AGENDA BE?

I would recommend that the formal meeting should take place followed by a site inspection. If there are specific sub meetings required to address specific items then these can be held afterwards with those parties that need to be there for that item.

- **Introduction of the people involved.** Identify the roles and responsibilities of everyone involved and make sure that you generate a project contact list with names, emails and phone numbers. Normally these are already known but you may have new parties involved such as your kitchen fitters that will need to be introduced to the team.

- **Builders Progress Report.** Get the builder to provide a report on the progress of the works, this should include the following:

- Overall progress to programme. Is it on programme, if not what is being done to bring it back on programme?

- Works completed since the last meeting

- Works scheduled to be undertaken during the next period and specific issues that need to be highlighted (power shutdowns etc.)
- Outstanding information required
- **Commercial status.**
- Project finances – budget review
- Changes and variations
- **Review the project risk register.** Make sure that any items that have an impact on the project programme are addressed
- **Agree the date of the next meeting.**

I would advise that the commercial and financial matters relating to individual parties are not addressed at this meeting but done privately with each party separately.

RECORD KEEPING AND ADMINISTRATION

As with the pre-start meeting, a formal record of the meeting needs to be kept in your meeting notes, with the action points are clearly identified together with the dates that they need to be addressed and the person responsible for addressing them. Circulate these notes to all the attendees and any other party that needs to have a copy in a timely manner so they have adequate time to address the actions.

CONTRACT ADMINISTRATION AND COMMUNICATION

Maintaining a disciplined tight control of the project through the construction phase is essential if you want to avoid costs escalating and the project going into delay.

Make sure that you continue to retain a tight control of the correspondence, instructions, budget, change control procedures, information requests and the project risk registers.

You can start out on your project with good intentions and for a while maintain the records well but as activity heats up on site it is too easy to slip into a relaxed state, especially when things appear to be going well from your perspective – only to be suddenly hit with additional costs out of the blue!

PROJECT CHANGE PITFALLS

You have to make sure that all instructions are formally confirmed in writing and not verbally. There are a number of ways that you can get caught out, and it is worth being aware of what to look out for:

Instructions that are deemed as a project change or variation – these may not just be limited to the physical works but also the way that works are carried out. Make sure that any instruction given goes through the formal change process even if it has a nil cost or no impact to the programme. It is easier to have it in writing than suddenly get a bill at the end of the project for it.

Never ask of favours from the builder or any of his sub-contractors. Contractually (within the building contract) there will be a restriction on this and they will retain the right to charge you for it so don't do it. If you want something done that is fine but agree it formally through the contractual mechanisms.

Watch out for the builder "boosting" the contract. Boosting is an unofficial term in the trade where builders identify additional works to be done, They say that it needs to be done because it's a knock on effect of the works or whilst they are carrying out the works they spot other defects with your home that need to be addressed. You will find this bad practice especially where the builder has priced the works too keenly to win the job and then tries to create additional profit by adding jobs to the project. If the builder raises any additional works then they may have a valid point but always get them to put to you in writing: what the issue is, why it is needed, how much it will cost and what the effect is on the programme? Then make a formal decision and instruct it utilising the contract process. This will mean that should their work fail it will at least be covered by the defects liability and insurances for the main works. Never instruct works outside of the contract.

Don't do work yourself that the builder is responsible for doing. Firstly, the builder will not accept liability for them and they may also cause additional cost through re-working if not done right. There will be times, if not managed correctly, that you could fall foul of their failure that puts you at an inconvenience resulting in you getting involved where you shouldn't. This is something that I have witnessed a few times, for example, where deliveries are made or sub-contractors carry out work and the client is left clearing up the mess, disposing of rubbish etc. My advice would be not to do it, at least not immediately. Notify the builder and give him the opportunity to come and do it himself. If he is unable to respond then notify him in writing, confirm that you have given him the opportunity, that he has either declined or failed to respond then advise him that you will do it (or better still get someone else to do it) but the costs associated with it will be deducted from his project cost (stating what the value will be which must be fair and reasonable). Give him a reasonable time to respond. Then instruct the change formally as part of the contract. You should only do this in extreme circumstances however and I would not recommend that you get too familiar with this because it will affect your relationship with your builder. You should let the builder get on with the project as much as is reasonably responsible and without inconveniencing yourself or your family.

BUILDING CONTROL INSPECTIONS

When you submit your project plans for Building Regulation approval they will be accepted with a set of obligations for the local Building Control Officer to inspect the works at key stages during the construction to ensure that the works are built in accordance with the Building Regulations.

You need to be aware of what stages the Building Control Officer will require to inspect the works and make sure that your builder calls in the officer for these when the time arises and before the works are covered up, otherwise the inspector may require completed elements of work to be opened up to allow his inspection causing abortive works and programme delays.

WHAT ELEMENTS WILL BE INSPECTED?

The focus will be on the elements identified within the Building Regulations Approved Documents A-P and will include:

 foundation excavations

 completed foundations

- fire protection
- drainage systems
- damp proof courses and membrane
- brickwork and block work for walls
- thermal insulation to walls floors and roofs
- structural elements
- weather proofing
- flues and vents to appliances
- ventilation
- staircases, landings and galleries
- safety glazing
- facilities for disabled people
- sound proofing

The Inspections will also be used to check:

- suitable materials are used
- work covered by the Building Regulations is carried out to a reasonable standard

WHEN WILL THE BUILDING CONTROL OFFICER INSPECT?

There are up to nine mandatory inspections, although these may not all be relevant to your particular project so you will need to review with your project manager and builder to ascertain where they apply:

1. **Commencement.** This is the first statutory notification. They normally visit when the work starts. However, in certain circumstances they may agree not to inspect the site until a further notice is received.

2. **Excavation for foundations.** For conventional foundations the foundation trench should be dug, levelled and cleaned to remove ground water before asking for an inspection. For special foundations, such as a raft foundation or piled foundations, consultation will need to be made with the Building Control Officer to agree an inspection programme in advance of the works.

3. **Foundations constructed** e.g. concrete poured. Notice must be given when the concrete has been placed. It is advisable to have the corners of the building marked out to show the position of the walls on the foundations. The Building Control Officer will be looking to see that the walls will be positioned correctly on the concrete.

4. **Damp proof course laid.** The Building Control Officer must be notified before any damp proof course is covered up.

5. **Over-site ready for concreting** (with damp proof membrane laid if appropriate). For solid ground bearing floor slabs it is the hard-core, insulation and damp proof membrane that the Building Control Officer will inspect before concrete. Where suspended timber floors are to be installed the ground below the over-site concrete will need to be inspected before it is covered by the floor.

6. **Structural members.** Any structural members such as floor joists, roof timbers and steel beams will need to be inspected.

7. **Drainage.** These must be visible for checking layout and construction before they are covered up so the bedding, falls and layout can be verified. All drainage work should be

inspected. This includes foul and surface water drainage to the building.

8. **Drains testing.** You should test the drains prior to them being covered and also when the building is complete. The Building Control Officer will often inspect all or a sample of the drainage tests to ensure that they are watertight and free draining.

9. **Completion.** When the building work is fully complete (or for new buildings, before occupation).

It is common for the Building Control Officer to inspect more than one element on one visit. Inspections 1 and 2 often coincide, as do 4 and 5 and 7 and 9.

Inspections 2-6 will normally be carried out on the next working day after notice has been given to the inspector to attend site.

ISSUE OF THE BUILDING CERTIFICATE

Once the Building Control Officer has inspected all the relevant stages of work, and is satisfied that the works comply with the Building Regulations, the appropriate certificates have been provided and the their fees paid, a Completion Certificate will be issued.

ADDITIONAL INSPECTIONS

As well as these mandatory inspections, further inspections may also be required such as Fire Protection and the Reinforcement of Concrete Structures although are less likely to be required for residential works. In addition, an inspector may call unexpectedly at other times to check on the work as it progresses.

HOW TO BOOK A BUILDING INSPECTOR

I would generally recommend that you write the obligation to arrange for the inspector within the builders duties within the Building Contract. In most circumstances Building inspectors offer a same day inspection service as long as they receive the request by 9:30am. They will normally be out inspecting from about 10:00am and therefore difficult to get hold of after 9:30.

PHASED COMPLETION AND BENEFICIAL USE

Often, where project works are being carried out in your home, as areas are completed you will want to be able to start using them, especially if the works are being carried out in a number of rooms and you are decanting from one space to another as the project progresses. Similarly you will want to be able to use amenities such as the kitchen and bathroom during the works as well as services such as the plumbing, heating and electrics.

You should clearly establish the programme of how these works will be undertaken and at what point they are deemed to be "complete" within the project, when you can start using them and what happens if defects arise.

You will also want to make sure that the defects liability period is clearly defined. Is it from when you have the beneficial use and start using them, which may mean that different parts of your project have differently assigned dates that you need to keep track of, or is it that you have beneficial use but the defects liability period only commences from the overall completion and handover of the project? Either option may apply depending on the specific nature of your project but it is important to establish these details at the start and have them contractually recorded.

SNAGGING AND TESTING

As the project works or phased elements of the project are reaching completion a snagging inspection should be undertaken to identify the specific elements that need finishing off ready for handover and the necessary statutory testing of installations that should be undertaken.

SNAGGING

I would recommend that you initially ask the builder to undertake his own snagging list and then present it to you or your project manager, who can then review this on site and confirm it or draw to the builders attention any additional items that you identify that also need closure. This can then provide a clear list of works that can be closed out ready for the handover and allow the completion and handover process to run smoothly.

The snagging list should be clear and easily set out for ease of reference. It should state the location, the building element, what the defect / issue is, what needs to be done to rectify it and by whom. It would also be useful in some instances to add a photograph for further ease of reference.

Make sure that there is only one complete snagging list for the project. There may be different trades and suppliers involved but try to avoid them all having their own lists as invariably items will get missed or one party will think someone else is doing it and the works will not get completed on time.

As each snagging item is completed they should be formally inspected and signed off by the builder and the project manager or you as appropriate.

TESTING

Most building services installations will require an element of testing prior to handover. This can include Statutory Testing obligations and performance / operational testing.

Typical elements that will require Statutory Testing include:

- Electrical Fixed Wiring Testing: To the electrical intake and mains distribution, power and lighting circuits around your home. This should also include any items of earth bonding and earth protection and will need to be undertaken by an electrician who is certified and registered as an approved tester

- Gas Safe Gas installation Tests: To test the gas pipework distribution and appliances such as boilers, cookers and fires. Testing will need to be undertaken by a registered Gas Safe engineer

- Drainage Testing: This will normally be undertaken by the builder and witnessed by the Building Control Officer

Completed certificates will be provided for the tests and Inspections.

Other installations and systems that you have installed will have testing carried out to ensure that they are installed and operate correctly. This can be important if they have warranties associated with them. Typical installations include:

- Security and alarm systems
- Heating controls
- Lighting controls
- Satellite and cable systems
- Telephone systems

THE HANDOVER PROCESS

You should make the handover process a formal milestone in the project. It is a defining moment to signify the completion of the works on site, ending the construction phase and moving into the defects liability period. It is therefore important that the date is carefully recorded.

As with the pre-start and progress meetings this should be conducted as a formal meeting. I would recommend that it is more of a formality meeting and issues such as checking off snagging items and completing the project accounts are all done prior to the meeting, so there are no nasty last minute surprises.

WHEN TO HOLD THE HANDOVER MEETING

The handover should take place on the agreed completion date, or earlier if all parties are satisfied and the works are completed. If the works are not completed then the handover cannot go ahead. You should make this clear and remain firm on this and **you should not accept the handover until all of the snagging items are completed and signed off**.

WHO SHOULD ATTEND?

Any stakeholders with contracts completing should be in attendance. If you have employed a project manager then they can act as your agent in this respect but as it is the biggest milestone of the project you are probably going to want to be there.

WHAT SHOULD THE FORMAT AND AGENDA BE?

I know it's the end of the project but there is no reason to let your professional control of the project fall at the last hurdle. Make sure that you have a clear agenda along the following lines:

- **Inspection of the works and sign off of the snagging list.** A final run through to make sure that all the works are complete and you are satisfied with the project works.

- **Handover of the project documentation.** Receive the final set of 'as installed' drawings, test certificates and manufacturers warranties etc.

- **Training and demonstration of equipment and installations.** Make sure that you receive full training on how to use all the installations you have been provided with.

- **Sign off the project account.** Make sure the project costs are all agreed and ready for the final payment (excluding the retention).

- **Confirm arrangements for the defects liability period.** Make sure you know who to contact to address any defects should they arise.

- **Celebrate and enjoy the success of your project!**

RECORD KEEPING AND ADMINISTRATION

Make sure that you complete your project plan and store all your documentation in a safe place.

DEALING WITH POST COMPLETION ISSUES

During the defects liability period the builder will be required to address any defects that arise in so far that they have not been caused by the client during normal use.

As part of the handover process you should have agreed a process for dealing with these and the costs for these should be down to the builder to fund.

Make sure that you have got up to date contact information including landline telephone, mobile number and an email address. Agree reasonable timescales against which the builder responds. If you call the builder up every day for very minor bits and pieces then naturally he is soon going to be reluctant to keep responding.

If you keep him advised of issues and agree dates when he can return and pick up a number in one go this will be much more effective.

Naturally if there is a major issue such as a loss of power or a water leak then get on to the builder straight away so make sure you have the contact numbers that you know in the event of an emergency will be answered. Make sure you test the numbers when you are given them.

Don't let him give you a long list of his sub-contractors; plumbers, electricians and the like for you to respond to. The issues are still his responsibility to manage so don't do his work for him. Equally don't forget that the Building Contract is still live so don't ask his staff or sub-contractors to undertake additional works that could be considered as contract variations.

CELEBRATING YOUR PROJECT

If you have followed the advice within this book then I hope it has brought you great success and now that you are at the end of your project you are in the fantastic position where you can sit back, relax and enjoy the benefits of your hard work for years to come.

Don't forget that while you may have completed your project there will be many others looking to have works done to their homes. Make sure you share your experiences, help refer good builders, tradesmen and professionals that you have used just as you were looking for advice, support and references as you started out on your project.

And, of course, if you find yourself struggling with any aspect that I have covered in this book, please do not hesitate to contact me.

help@manageyourproject.co.uk

Well Done and I hope you enjoy the end result!

GLOSSARY OF TERMS

Scope – The extent of activities to be undertaken

Tradesmen – Skilled workforce to be utilised in carrying out the project works, builders, bricklayers, plumbers, electricians, carpenters etc.

Fixtures – The fixed elements of the building works including doors, windows, dado rails, skirting's, built in wardrobes and cupboards, architectural features, kitchen units and worktops.

Fittings – The additional items that fit to fixtures such as ironmongery (door handles, latches, locks), power sockets, light switches and light holders, kitchen appliances, taps, plugs, shower curtains, shelving.

Contract / Building Contract – The formal agreement between the client and the builder

Contractual Variation / Change – an amendment made to the agreed building contract.

Project Risk –an aspect of the project that has the potential to prevent the project meeting its objective, be it time, cost or quality. Project risks can be identified any point in a project from design, construction and post completion.

Financial Risk – where a project cost may remain unresolved such as outstanding instruction of provisional sums, additional project costs due to unknown events.

Architect – The design team member trained to plan and design the building

Quantity Surveyor – The project team member responsible for the financial accounting of the project, establishing the project costs and if appropriate managing the ongoing project budget.

Architectural Draftsmen – prepares detailed technical drawings for building construction, normally works under an architect.

Structural Engineer – the design team member trained to ensure the structural integrity and soundness of the construction.

Building Services Engineer – the design team member responsible for the design and specification of the building services which incorporate the drainage, rainwater disposal, hot and cold water services, heating, electrical power, lighting, fire alarms, security systems.

Interior Designers – the design team member responsible for creating the functional and aesthetic use of the space within a building

Planning Permission – The statutory consent required from the Local Authority for demolition and building on land or change of use of land

Planning Approval – The consent given as the statutory consent required from the Local Authority for demolition and building on land or change of use of land

Project Status – the point where the project is against the defined measurable of the project in respect of time or cost.

Building Regulations – The Statutory standards which works are to be built to.

Construction Design & Management Regulations – Statutory Regulations governing the management of health & safety in the construction industry.

Planning Officer – The Local Authority representative responsible for managing the Planning Application process.

Planning Authority / Department – The department within the Local authority responsible for the management of the Planning application process.

Building Control – the department within the local Authority responsible for ensuring building works are compliant with the Building regulations.

Party Wall Agreement – The Statutory licence required with adjoining property owners accepting the structural integrity of the project works in association with their property.

Risk Register – The document used to manage, control and report the project risks.

Milestones – The key points within a project programme used to monitor progress.

Criteria – The value or level of content that is required to be met.

Duty of Care – The legal obligation imposed on an individual or party requiring that they adhere to a standard of reasonable consideration while performing an act, principally considered in respect of health & safety.

Tender – A procurement process where bidders are invited to submit a priced proposal for undertaking works or services.

Method Statement – a description detailing the procedure to be adopted to undertake an item of work or service.

Due Diligence – The research and validation exercise undertaken to evaluate and confirm information provided.

Schedule of Condition – A listing of the state of an element or building identifying any existing defects, level of decoration and completeness.

Procurement – the process of buying an item or service.

Liability – legal responsibility for something, especially costs or damages

Sub-contracting – the use of a third party to provide goods or services on their behalf by the contracted party

Dispute – a disagreement between two contracted parties

Incident Planning – The management process put in place to prepare in the event of an unplanned event occurring.

Snagging – the checking of works and identification of defects to be repaired, replaced or completed.

Fixed cost – A set non-adjustable value for defined goods or services.

Estimate – an approximate cost or allowance for goods or services.

Provisional Sum – a budget cost placed in the project cost plan for a service or goods the details of which are yet to be defined.

Project Contingency – a budget cost placed in the project budget that is not allocated to any specific item or service but is provided to address any unknown items or incidents that arise during the course of the project.

Prelims – The costs incurred by the builder that are not specific to the physical construction, these typically include site accommodation, welfare facilities, storage, security, site management, health & safety systems and training.

Retentions – Monies within the overall project costs for construction that are held back from payment to the builder for an agreed period of time after completion to deal with any defects or repairs that may be required.

Defects Liability – a set period of time after the construction project has been completed during which a contractor has the obligation to return to site to address any defects

Project Account – The funds from which the costs of the building works are paid from.

Beneficial Use – The use by the client of either partially completed or an element of phased completion of the project works before the completion date.

Permissions & Approvals – the two primary legal terms for acceptance, principally in respect of planning and building control.

Novation / Novated – To substitute the services of one party for another, in this context it is appointing one contractor to be used by another.

FURTHER RESOURCES

The Planning Portal – The Government site providing advice and information relating to the planning process.
http://www.planningportal.gov.uk/planning/

Department for Communities and Local Government – www.communities.gov.uk

Federation of Master Builders – www.fmb.org.uk

Gase Safe Register – www.gassaferegister.co.uk

Health & Safety Executive – www.hse.gov.uk

National House Building Council (NHBC) – www.nhbc.co.uk

National Self Build & Renovation Centre – www.buildstore.co.uk

Royal institute of Chartered Surveyors (RICS) – www.rics.org

Royal institute of British Architects (RIBA) – www.architecture.com

ABOUT THE AUTHOR

David has been in the construction industry since he left school some 30 years ago. Originally he trained as an engineer but moved into project and building management. He has been involved in a large range of construction projects including museums, galleries, hospitals, data centres, offices and call centres as well as residential works.

Now the owner of The Residential Project Manager Limited, David spends most of his time helping home owners and property developers to deliver a mixture of loft conversions, extensions, refurbishments and new builds. Having been in the commercial industry for a long time he now enjoys helping local people deliver their dreams.

David was raised and still lives in Hemel Hempstead in Hertfordshire and is married to his wife Sue and has two teenage boys George & Harry.

You know that thing you always wanted to do?

Well maybe it isn't too late after all!

"Twenty-one came and went and although the dream was still there (floating, less bright but still alive, somewhere behind a stack of stress and hidden amidst a sea of overtime hours in a distant corner of his mind) Charlie barely noticed that his dreamline-deadline had ticked its final tock."

Well maybe it isn't too late after all!

"You see Charlie believed that he was going to be successful. He believed that he was special and that one day he would rise above the mass of mediocrity which surrounded him, dragged him down and slowly drained him of his ambition; and then he would make a name for himself."

The Lazy Optimist tells the story of an everyday man who had been harbouring the embers of potential in his heart for far too long. It is a tale of hope and describes how he managed to escape his life of genuine optimism, held back by fear, cunningly disguised as bad luck and resulting in a kind of directionless, busy-laziness...

And if Charlie can...

ISBN: 978-1-906954-72-7	Format: Paperback
Published: 13 April 2013	RRP: £7.99

If you found this book useful, you will also be interested in Clive's first book...

How To Franchise Your Business

The plain speaking guide for business owners

by Clive Sawyer

Available from Amazon and www.liveitpublishing.com

"Essential reading for business owners considering franchising their business."

Richard Holden, Head of Franchising, Lloyds Banking Group

Clive Sawyer, Managing Director of Business Options, one of the UK's leading Franchise and Business Expansion Consultancies, has written this book to cut through the confusion and complexity surrounding franchising a business.

Clive, in his renowned plain speaking manner helps the reader assess whether franchising is the right expansion model for them. He then leads the reader, step by step through everything they will need to know.

For anyone serious about franchising their business, this book is essential reading.

Printed in Great Britain
by Amazon